"Michael Gorman has  tten an eminently readable int¨ minish-es the apostle's practical ¨icates the profound depth of P ¨s they are challenging. *Reading* ¨serves the widest possible readership."

—Joel B. Green, Professor of New Testament Interpretation, Fuller Theological Seminary

"Michael Gorman, already established as a perceptive and creative interpreter of Paul's letters, now offers us a user-friendly introduction to Paul the person. Gorman's book aptly fulfills the Companions series goal. He makes Paul our contemporary 'companion' by introducing major themes from Paul's letters in such a personal way. I warmly recommend this book to pastors, seminarians, and anyone interested in getting to know Paul better!"

—Fr. Ronald D. Witherup, SS, Provincial Superior of the U.S. Province of Sulpicians

"Reading Paul well means reading Paul specifically as Christian Scripture, 'the voice of God speaking to us,' to use Michael Gorman's phrase. In this book, Gorman not only reads Paul well, he exemplifies a passion for helping others in the Church to do so. He elegantly weaves historical, social, and political aspects of Paul's context into a powerful theological reading of the apostle's letters that reverberates with contemporary implications for the church in North America. His lucid exposition of justification as grace-enabled co-crucifixion and co-resurrection with Christ demonstrates keen exegetical and theological acumen and is worth the price of the book. Its clarity and engaging style make it easy to recommend for local church groups and classes where Paul is the focus."

—Andy Johnson, Professor of New Testament, Nazarene Theological Seminary

"An already established expert on Paul, Gorman now offers the eager but uninitiated reader an accessible and illuminating overview of the apostle's writings, theology and spirituality. Here is a 'big picture' perspective which invites and enables the reader to envisage, enter into, and enjoy Scripture speaking to us and for God."

—S. A. Cummins, Director, MA in Biblical Studies, Trinity Western University

Reading Paul

Cascade Companions

The Christian theological tradition provides an embarrassment of riches: from scripture to modern scholarship, we are blessed with a vast and complex theological inheritance. And yet this feast of traditional riches is too frequently inaccessible to the general reader.

The Cascade Companions series addresses the challenge by publishing books that combine academic rigor with broad appeal and readability. They aim to introduce nonspecialist readers to that vital storehouse of authors, documents, themes, histories, arguments, and movements that comprise this heritage with brief yet compelling volumes.

TITLES IN THIS SERIES:

Reading Augustine by Jason Byassee

Conflict, Community, and Honor by John H. Elliott

An Introduction to the Desert Fathers by Jason Byassee

FORTHCOMING TITLES:

Theology and Culture: A Guide to the Discussion by D. Stephen Long

iPod, YouTube, Wii Play: Theological Engagements with Entertainment by Brent Laytham

Creationism and Evolution by Tatha Wiley

Theological Interpretation of Scripture by Stephen Fowl

Reading Paul

Michael J. Gorman

CASCADE *Books* • Eugene, Oregon

READING PAUL

Cascade Companions

Cascade Books
A Division of Wipf and Stock Publishers
199 W. 8th Ave., Suite 3
Eugene, OR 97401

ISBN13: 978-1-55635-195-2

Cataloging-in-Publication data:

Gorman, Michael J., 1955–

Reading Paul / Michael J. Gorman.

x + 196 p.; 20 cm.

Cascade Companions

ISBN13: 978-1-55635-195-2

1. Bible. N.T. Epistles of Paul—Theology. 2. Bible. N.T. Epistles of Paul—Criticism, interpretation, etc. 3. Paul, The Apostle, Saint. I. Title II. Series.

BS2651 G64 2008

Contents

Acknowledgments

✣ I am grateful to Jon Stock of Wipf and Stock Publishers for the invitation to contribute this volume to the Cascade Companions series. Special thanks go to those who read and commented on the manuscript, in whole or in part, before its publication. Among these were two New Testament colleagues and fellow Pauline scholars, Andy Johnson and Ron Witherup. I cannot adequately express my gratitude to Andy Johnson in particular; without his careful comments on every chapter, this book would be much poorer. My graduate students and research assistants, Lenore Turner and Bob Anderson, suggested improvements to the manuscript. Lenore also meticulously checked the Scripture references.

In addition, the book was "road-tested" with representatives of the intended audiences: motivated lay people and beginning students of Paul. These include my wife Nancy; several fellow-members of Community United Methodist Church and my adult-education class there: Mike Cantley, John Gurney, Adam Nucci, and Nelson Outten; two dear friends, Marilyn and Joe Murchison, with whom I have read Scripture and prayed for nearly two decades; plus one of my children, Brian, a college student, and his Kenyan friend Gordon Odira, a recent college graduate. All of their comments were invaluable, but I am especially grateful for the insights of Mike, a budding pastoral theologian and peacemaker; Adam, a very careful reader; and Joe, a superb writer and editor.

My debt to other interpreters of the apostle is too large to acknowledge in full here, but I will mention two names whose strong influence will be evident: Richard B. Hays of Duke Divinity School and N. T. (Tom) Wright, Bishop of Durham in the Church of England. It is a great privilege to count them both also as friends, though of course I hold neither of them, nor anyone else, responsible for any mistakes I have made in the interpretation of our mutual friend, Paul.

Unless otherwise indicated, all biblical quotations are taken from the New Revised Standard Version (NRSV).

I wrote some of these words while on a visit to the ecumenical Christian community in Taizé France, which is dedicated to unity, reconciliation, and peace through Christ. Taizé music helps many, myself included, to implement the Pauline exhortation to pray without ceasing. In addition, Taizé is a peaceable community and movement of which Paul would be proud and, I think, part.

October 3, 2007

1

Why Paul?

Of the making of books on the apostle Paul there is no end. I have scores of them on my bookshelves, and there are hundreds more in my seminary's library. I have written two such books myself, plus a Ph.D. dissertation—a total of nearly 2,000 pages. Most of my professional colleagues in biblical studies have written, or are writing, at least one book on Paul. So why yet another, especially one for serious lay readers, beginning students, and those who are not immediately attracted to Paul?

Before answering that question, we should pause to consider the context in which we read and write about Paul. If the first decade is any indication, the twenty-first century will be an era characterized by new forms of both imperialism and tribalism, each marked by violence and, often, motivated by religious commitments. In fact, some influential voices suggest that religion is the problem.[1] And of course Paul is a religious figure. So is Paul part of the problem?

While the global situation is marked by quests for domination and by bitter divisions, the situation in many Christian churches seems to be a microcosm of the larger world, minus (usually) the violence. Since the name of Paul is often invoked

1. E.g., Harris, *The End of Faith* and *Letter to a Christian Nation*; Dawkins, *The God Delusion*.

on both sides of a debate or rift, we wonder again, Is Paul part of the problem?

Not in my view. I think that we can, and must, read Paul as our contemporary, and as Scripture.

Reading Paul's Letters as Scripture

The answer to "Why another book on Paul?" lies in my conviction that too many books, even the best ones, treat him only as an ancient figure, not as our companion and contemporary, much less a conduit of divine revelation. The extreme version of this view is implied in the following quotation from the perspective of the social sciences:

> Modern Christianity in all its forms has little to do with its ancestral expressions in the Jesus groups of Paul's day, as we hope our commentary will demonstrate.[2]

The authors of this sentence are rightly trying to help their readers enter the world of the first century and not impose their own situations on first-century documents. But they do so at great expense, losing Paul as a spiritual guide. They abandon the very reason Paul interests people in the first place: what he said to "Jesus groups" then he says also to Christians today. Paul's writings, after all, are Christian *Scripture*. They are part of the Christian Bible, which is recognized by Christians as the primary authority for our knowledge of God and the primary instrument of God's ongoing address to the Christian community.[3]

2. Malina and Pilch, *Letters of Paul*, 3.

3. This is a fairly generic interpretation of the word "Scripture," intended to encompass a wide range of positions on the Bible's import for Christians.

Thus I want to read Paul, and help others read Paul, as Scripture, as—to be blunt—the voice of God speaking to us. This approach is obviously quite different from that of the social sciences. It is even different from some allegedly theological readings that stress the fact that Paul writes about God but say nothing of how Paul brings the word of God to us. My approach assumes, as Joel Green has eloquently argued, that we are part of the same community to which Paul's first recipients belonged—the church universal.[4] Green says:

> The first question, then [in the interpretation of the Bible as Scripture], is not what separates us (language, diet, worldview, politics, social graces, and so forth) from the biblical authors, but whether we are ready to embrace the God to whom and the theological vision to which these writers bear witness.[5]

He continues:

> [I]n the same way that to refer to the Bible as Scripture is a theological statement, to speak of the church, theologically, is to speak of its oneness across time and space. There is only one people of God.
>
> That is, *historical* judgments about the audience of a biblical text stand in tension with the *theological* affirmation of the oneness of the church that receives this biblical text *as Scripture*. Historical criticism assumes what Christians can never assume—namely, that there is more than one people of God.[6]

4. Green, *Seized by Truth*, especially 50–62.
5. Ibid., 18.
6. Ibid., 51.

That is, the writers and readers of Scripture constitute one community of faith.

To be sure, there is merit in remembering that Paul and his letter-recipients lived in a culture different from our own. We need to acknowledge the distance between now and then, and we need to employ tools to understand "then."[7] But the perspective that stresses difference should not be the governing view we bring to the reading of Paul. If it is, we betray the apostle's own purpose in writing and forget the very meaning of the word "Scripture." It is especially ironic that so many professional scholars of Paul continue to distance him from us when even people *outside* the church and *outside* the guild of biblical scholars—for instance, European political philosophers—find Paul of great contemporary value.[8]

This is not to disparage historical study but to place it in a broader interpretive framework. This book assumes that we read Paul best when we read him speaking *to* us and *for* God. We need to read him as an apostle and prophet—as most people inside the Christian church have traditionally done. If readers seek other approaches, there are many good books to satisfy them, and those books can also help people who read Paul as Scripture. But if readers are at least willing to try this approach, they may find it no less responsible, and far more satisfying, than the "objective" approaches that ignore Paul's claim to speak the word of God.

I am well aware that many people are less than certain that Paul speaks for God. There are at least two major reasons

7. As Green says (*Seized by Truth*, 24), "[T]he practices of interpretation that have arisen since the late 1700s are not thereby cast aside, but they are dethroned."

8. See, for example, Badiou, *Saint Paul: The Foundation of Universalism.*

for this hesitation. First, Christians follow Jesus, not Paul, and we find Jesus in the Gospels rather than in the letters of Paul. Jesus proclaimed the world-changing arrival of God's kingdom, while Paul only preached "justification by faith," or so it is often thought. Thus, some think, Christians should major in the gospels and minor, at best, in Paul, whereas many Christians, especially Protestants, have done just the opposite. Moreover, some people believe that those who focus on Paul have turned his writings into a source of theological ideas, such as justification, that often seem irrelevant to everyday life or the great social problems of our day. Second, many people find in Paul other ideas that seem offensive to postmodern ears—his alleged disdainful view of women, condemnation of homosexuals, conservative politics and unquestioning support of authority, exclusivist tendencies, and arrogance. If this list is a fair summary of Paul's views, he could justifiably be seen as part of the problem.

It would take an entire book to address these two concerns—irrelevance and offense—fully. But two quick rejoinders may be helpful. First, Paul is not as distant from Jesus as he might, at first glance, appear. The kingdom of God in Jesus' teaching was about the universal reign of Israel's God and the creation of a new community embodying God's covenant and character by living together as Jesus' disciples. So, too, with Paul, except that his experience of the *resurrected* Jesus led him to reframe the message of God's reign as the lordship of Jesus, God's Son and Messiah, and of life *in* him. In the context of first-century Rome (and of twenty-first-century superpowers), both Jesus and Paul proclaimed, in word and deed, the "empire" of God.[9] Whatever else justification means, it means participation in the life of this one God of the covenant who reigns supreme and deserves our loyalty.

Second, Paul may be both less and more offensive than he is normally thought to be. A new approach to Paul that takes his radical gospel seriously will have to re-examine the common understandings of his views on controversial matters. He may, for instance, be far less politically and socially "conservative" than we think. Yet he may also be far less "tolerant" on some issues than we want. The purpose of this book is not to settle all those difficult aspects of Paul,[10] but to provide a wider framework for understanding and grappling with them.

This book, then, is a guide to reading Paul. As such it is not a traditional "introduction," though it touches on many subjects covered in such works.[11] Rather, after this preliminary chapter, there are three chapters on Paul, his letters, and his gospel. The book is then organized around eight themes that lie in and behind his letters.[12] Understanding these essential themes will allow the reader to hear them as they echo throughout the letters and, I trust, to be caught up in them as the living and active word of God. A short final chapter attempts to synthesize that word spoken *through* Paul and *to* us.

This does not mean that we will never struggle with Paul's letters, and we may even debate with the apostle. His

9. See, e.g., Horsley and Silberman, *The Message and the Kingdom*.

10. This book is not an attempt to "liberate" Paul. For such an effort, with mixed results, see Elliott, *Liberating Paul*.

11. My contribution to this genre of book is *Apostle of the Crucified Lord*.

12. For this reason, this book can also be called a theology of Paul.

contemporaries certainly did, and within about a generation people were already misunderstanding and even abusing Paul's letters, because like the rest of the Scriptures they are hard to understand (2 Pet 3:15–16). But just as a purely historical perspective should not govern our reading of Paul, neither should an antagonistic one. Yes, Paul has been and can be misused, but Paul has been and can be trusted—trusted to speak for God and to light a fire of understanding and devotion among those who read his letters.

Some readers will be aware that there is scholarly dispute about which of the thirteen New Testament letters attributed to Paul were actually written by him and which were, or may have been, written by his "disciples" a generation or so later. Seven of the thirteen are called the "undisputed letters" (Romans, 1 and 2 Corinthians, Galatians, Philippians, 1 Thessalonians, Philemon) because scholars agree almost universally that they come from Paul.[13] This book is based largely on the undisputed letters, with some backup support from the disputed correspondence.[14]

Paul in One Sentence

Some readers of this book will also wonder about its particular "take" on Paul: "old school," "new perspective," "post-new perspective," "fresh perspective," or what? My work on Paul defies easy classification. It will be better to begin with a

---

13. It should be noted that some, but not all, of the most difficult passages in the Pauline correspondence come from the disputed letters.

14. My own view, described in chapter three, is that Paul is more or less responsible for all of the disputed letters except 1 Timothy and Titus.

glimpse of Paul's grand scheme as I see it, doing so in one long sentence, as follows:

> Paul preached, and then explained in various pastoral, community-forming letters, a narrative, apocalyptic, theopolitical gospel (1) in continuity with the story of Israel and (2) in distinction to the imperial gospel of Rome (and analogous powers) that was centered on God's crucified and exalted Messiah Jesus, whose incarnation, life, and death by crucifixion were validated and vindicated by God in his resurrection and exaltation as Lord, which inaugurated the new age or new creation in which all members of this diverse but consistently cove-nantally dysfunctional human race who respond in self-abandoning and self-committing faith thereby participate in Christ's death and resurrection and are (1) justified, or restored to right covenant rela-tions with God and with others; (2) incorporated into a particular manifestation of Christ the Lord's body on earth, the church, which is an alternative community to the status-quo human communities committed to and governed by Caesar (and analo-gous rulers) and by values contrary to the gospel; and (3) infused both individually and corporately by the Spirit of God's Son so that they may lead "bifocal" lives, focused both back on Christ's first coming and ahead to his second, consisting of Christlike, cruciform (cross-shaped) (1) faith and (2) hope toward God and (3) love toward both neighbors and enemies (a love marked by peace-ableness and inclusion), in joyful anticipation of (1) the return of Christ, (2) the resurrection of the dead to eternal life, and (3) the renewal of the entire creation.

This complex sentence—complex in terms of both structure and content—will make much more sense by the end of the book. In fact, I would urge readers to return to this sentence after they have digested its contents in the chapters that follow.

Summary

Why read Paul in our context? As a Christian, I read Paul, and I invite others to read him, because his letters are Scripture. But I will also contend in this book that when we unpack the long sentence printed above, we find that Paul speaks powerfully to the life-threatening, violent imperialism and tribalism of this century and of any century.[15]

Reflection

1. What comes to mind when you hear or read the term "Scripture"?

2. How would you describe the context in which you read Paul?

3. Which aspects of Paul and his letters have you found inspired and inspiring?

4. Which aspects have you found troublesome, and why?

---

15. Three dimensions of Paul's experience and thought receive more focused attention here than in my earlier books: the resurrection, multiculturalism, and peacemaking/nonviolence.

"Grace and Apostleship"

Conversion, Call, Commission

✣ It had never occurred to me to compare the apostle Paul to the Rev. Dr. Martin Luther King Jr. But one Sunday, on the January weekend when Americans commemorate Dr. King, the children's sermon at church rehearsed the life of the civil rights leader, and I could not help but notice the similarities between his story and Paul's. Like Dr. King, Paul knew himself to be commissioned by God to preach and live a socially and politically charged message that

- focused on the justice of God;
- called for the inclusion of outsiders in the beloved community;
- necessitated the rejection of violence;
- implicitly, and sometimes explicitly, challenged imperial power;
- meant living in the shadow of the cross and the power of the resurrection; and
- resulted in much persecution, and eventually death.

This list suggests both the parallels between Paul and Dr. King and the shape of Paul's life itself after his encounter with the resurrected Jesus. Prior to that experience, Paul was a far cry from either Dr. King or the man that the encounter birthed.

Zealous for God, Enemy of the Church

We know relatively little of Paul's life before his encounter with Jesus. He was probably a younger contemporary of the provocative prophet from Nazareth, born between about 5 BC and AD 10—more likely later in that range. Acts tells us that he was a zealous Pharisee (Acts 23:6; 26:5) from the city of Tarsus[1] (Acts 9:11; 21:39; 22:3) but had been educated also in Jerusalem under the prominent rabbi Gamaliel (Acts 22:3). Acts relates that Paul spoke both Greek (Acts 21:37), the common language of the Mediterranean region, and Aramaic (Acts 21:40; 22:2 ["Hebrew"]), the mother tongue of Palestinian Jews. Several times Acts reports that he was a Roman citizen (Acts 16:37–38; 22:25–29; 23:27).

Paul's own letters confirm that he was a Pharisee, proud of his heritage and his zeal for the Law of God (Phil 3:4–6; Gal 1:13–14). The Pharisees were the Jewish "party" that felt called to maintain the purity of Israel through adherence to the Law. Unlike some Jews, such as the Sadducees, they affirmed the coming general resurrection of the dead, a conviction that Paul shared but would have to completely reinterpret once he became convinced that God had already raised Jesus of Nazareth from the dead.

Although the letters do not mention Paul's birthplace, education, or citizenship, these are all plausible data. Also plausible is his possession of two names, the Jewish name

1. Capital of the Roman province of Cilicia, in what is now southeastern Turkey.

Saul, appropriate for a Benjaminite,[2] and the Roman name Paul. His letters, written in Greek, confirm his thorough knowledge of that language but also, at least, his familiarity with some Aramaic words used in the early churches (*abba*, "Father": Rom 8:15; Gal 4:6; *maranatha*, "Our Lord, come": 1 Cor 16:22).

The most important aspect of Paul's pre-Jesus life is narrated vividly by both Acts and the Pauline letters: his zeal as a Pharisee led him to want to destroy the church of God (Acts 7:54—8:1; 9:1–4; 1 Cor 15:9; Gal 1:13; Phil 3:6), the movement of Jews and Gentiles who believed that the crucified Jesus—a failed messianic fraud, in Paul's eyes—had been raised from the dead by God and was therefore the Messiah of Israel, Savior of the world, and Lord of the universe. This dangerous lie Paul could not tolerate.

The combination of zealous religiosity and violence is something with which we are all too familiar today. For Paul, it was both a badge of honor and a mandate from God, which sounds eerily familiar. The earliest Christian movement was really a group within Judaism—and for Paul it was a defilement of his religion and people. The movement worshipped a crucified criminal (who should have been viewed as cursed by God, not blessed),[3] allegedly vindicated in resurrection, and supposedly exalted to heaven. Moreover, the movement played loose with the Law of God, manifested especially in its apparently unqualified openness to Gentiles. Such inclu-

2. Rom 11:1; Phil 3:5. Benjamin was one of Jacob's twelve sons and thus head of one of the twelve tribes of Israel. Israel's first king and Paul's namesake, Saul, was from this tribe.

3. See Deut 21:23, cited in Gal 3:13.

sion compromised the purity of the covenant people, which a zealous Pharisee could not permit. Thus the two main reasons (no doubt there were others) Paul wanted to eliminate the fledgling church were (1) its preaching of a crucified, cursed Messiah and (2) its embrace of Gentiles in a way that polluted Israel.

Paul had precedent both for his concern and for his conviction that God would want the problem remedied with violence, if necessary. Israel had a history of holy heroes whose zeal for God motivated their taking violent action against Israel's enemies and even against Israel itself. The most well-known of these is Elijah (1 Kings 18), but perhaps the most important precedent for Paul was Phinehas, the grandson of Aaron. Although the name of Phinehas does not appear in the New Testament, his figure casts a long shadow over Paul's pre-Damascus life. According to Numbers 25, Phinehas was so full of zeal that he killed an Israelite man and his Midianite consort to purify the people from the immorality and idolatry introduced into the community by non-Israelites. Phinehas was rewarded with divine approval and a perpetual priesthood (Num 25:10–13). He was even celebrated in a psalm, which says that his violent act was "reckoned to him as righteousness" (Ps 106:30–31).

If that language sounds Pauline, it is (Rom 4:3–11, 22–24; Gal 3:6). But it is borrowed from Gen 15:6, which speaks of Abraham's faith being reckoned to him as righteousness. There are only two figures in Israel's Scriptures about whom it is said that something was "reckoned to him as righteousness": Abraham and Phinehas. Before Damascus, Paul found in Phinehas the paradigm of righteousness.[4]

So Paul was fulfilling his obligation as a Pharisee to promote the Law and protect Israel from impurity by seeking to wipe out the new movement before it spread like cancer. He believed that this zeal, like that of Phinehas, was the basis of his right relationship with God—his justification. But this violent and exclusivist impulse would be challenged and, nonviolently, overthrown.

The Encounter with Jesus

Both Acts and Paul's letters describe Paul's unexpected and unmerited (1 Cor 15:9–10) encounter with the resurrected Jesus, some time in the mid-thirties of the first century. Although Acts gives more details, Paul supplies the essentials, saying that the resurrected Jesus appeared to him as he had previously done to others, apparently one of the chief criteria for apostleship (1 Cor 9:1; 15:8). This was a divine revelation, an *apokalypsis* (Gal 1:15–16), the defining moment of Paul's life. From this experience sprang much of Paul's theology, as his belief system was first rocked and then reformulated by this seismic event, when Paul was apprehended (Phil 3:12) by the one whose people he would have apprehended. He abandoned his former, violent zeal for a zeal for the Lord defined by accepting rather than inflicting suffering (Rom 12:12, 14). The following table shows some aspects of Paul's "180":

4. Paul would later see Abraham as the model of righteousness (Romans 4; Galatians 3) and find the zeal of his fellow Jews misguided (Rom 10:2).

Before the appearance of Jesus to him, Paul	After the appearance of Jesus to him, Paul
rejected the cross and the crucified one	embraced the cross and the crucified one
denied Jesus' resurrection	affirmed Jesus' resurrection
dissociated God from Jesus and Jesus from messiahship	associated God with Jesus and Jesus with messiahship
excluded Gentiles, as Gentiles, from the covenant people	included Gentiles who embraced Jesus, as Gentiles, in the covenant people
focused on the Torah	focused on the Messiah
sought Israel's purity and his own justification through violent zeal	sought Israel's purpose and his own justification through the loving obedience of the Son of God and his participation in it
opposed and sought the destruction of the Jesus-is-Messiah movement	affirmed and joined the Jesus-is-Messiah movement, sought its universal expansion, and willingly suffered for it

It should surprise no one that Paul, the onetime persecutor, understood what happened to him as *grace*, God's unmerited favor (1 Cor 15:10), which would become the cornerstone of his theology (Romans 5; cf. Eph 2:8–10). It may surprise some, however, that there are scholars who do not like to refer to his experience as a conversion. That resistance is primarily because the word "conversion" often implies a change of religions, say, from Judaism to Christianity.[5] And Paul did

5. The classic example of this resistant position is Stendahl, *Paul*

not convert in that sense. He remained a Jew but became a radically different kind of Jew: one convinced that the crucified Jesus had in fact been resurrected by Israel's God and was therefore Messiah and Lord. Paul was now a "messianic Jew."

Yet not to call Paul's experience a conversion is to deny the proverbial elephant in the room. Paul did what sociologists say a conversion entails: he changed convictions, conduct, and community.[6] And he expected those whose conversion he facilitated to do the same.

Called and Commissioned

Paul's experience, however, was more than a conversion; it was also a prophetic call and a commission. Paul deliberately recounts the event with echoes of the call narratives of the prophets, especially Jeremiah (Gal 1:15; see Jer 1:5; cf. Isa 49:5). Like the prophets, Paul believed that God had called him to a specific task. His was to preach the good news of Jesus especially among the Gentiles—the very ones whose inclusion had stirred him to violence.

The primary title associated with this commission is "apostle," someone sent with the authority of the sender, a kind of ambassador (2 Cor 5:20). The apostolic title appears in the first verse of nine of the thirteen Pauline letters. When Paul speaks or writes, people listen—or at least he expects them to do so. But Paul had to struggle to prove his apostolic office. He had been a persecutor, so he was suspect for years. Furthermore, he refused financial support from those he evangelized, which

---

Among Jews and Gentiles.

6. See Segal, *Paul the Convert.* The change of community does *not*, however, mean rejection of Israel.

was probably seen as disobedience to Jesus (Luke 10:7) and contrary to normal apostolic practice (1 Cor 9:3–14). So too, perhaps, was his singleness (1 Cor 7:7; 9:5). Beyond that, he was not a very "charismatic" speaker (2 Cor 10:10). When he exerted his apostolic authority in absentia (1 Cor 5:3–5), or threatened to come as a disciplining father (1 Cor 4:14–21), he may not have been appreciated as God's envoy.

But "apostle" did not mean "bully" or even primarily "authority figure." It meant "father," "mother," "pastor," "example," and especially "Christ-bearer." We will consider these images briefly in the next chapter.

The Consequences of the Encounter

We have already noted some of the consequences of Paul's about-face. But we need now to return especially to the aspects of this experience that parallel the life of Martin Luther King Jr., especially nonviolence and reconciliation/inclusion.

It is easy to think of Paul as a preacher or pastor, even as an example. It is more difficult for us to see him as a critic of empire or a peacemaker, much less a pacifist. Yet the turn to nonviolence is at the very heart of Paul's conversion, and his gospel. Paul's pacifism, as we will see further in chapter 11, was rooted in his gospel's proclamation of how God in Christ had treated enemies and insurgents against the divine order with reconciling, suffering love (Rom 3:9–26; 5:6–11; 2 Cor 5:18–19). This nonviolent divine love was then manifested in Paul's own practice of absorbing violence without retaliation (1 Cor 4:10–13) and communicated to his churches as the only appropriate lifestyle for those converted by and to the love of God (1 Thess 5:15; Rom 12:9–21). Once again, we see the parallels between Paul and Dr. King. We do not hear the whole gospel according to Paul—or perhaps we do not hear it at all—if we do not hear this essential dimension. Nonviolence is not negotiable for Paul the convert and apostle.

In Paul's day, Jewish zealous nationalism that focused on Israel's internal purity was not the only temptation to violence. That nationalistic zeal was also directed outwardly, toward an oppressive, violent regime—the imperial power of Rome.[7] Paul would become a critic (at least an implicit one) of that form of violence, too—violence in the name of justice, peace, and security. Based on a misinterpretation of Rom 13:1–7, Paul is often portrayed as a political conservative who supported Rome, and perhaps all forms of political authority, even tyranny. However, like Jesus, he was a critic of imperial values such as domination and of imperial claims like divine status for emperors and divine blessing on the empire's ambition.[8] Paul mocked the Roman claim of providing *pax et securitas* (1 Thess 5:3), offered an alternative form of divine justice, and proclaimed as Lord a criminal crucified by Roman power—rather than Roman power incarnate (the emperor). A politics of subversion, not intentional but as an inevitable consequence of the gospel, is central to Paul and to those who read his letters as Scripture. In that sense, Paul was a good, prophetic Jew.

7. There were numerous large and small Jewish uprisings against Rome in the first century—all crushed by Roman might, with leaders and participants often punished by crucifixion.

8. The literature on this is vast. See, for example, Wright, *Paul: In Fresh Perspective*, 59–79; Wright, "Paul's Gospel and Caesar's Empire"; Horsley, ed., *Paul and Empire*; and Crossan and Reed, *In Search of Paul*. See further discussion in chapter 8.

Another essential consequence of Paul's conversion was his inclusion of Gentiles in the "beloved community." They did not need to become Jews (through circumcision; see Galatians 5) in order to be grafted onto the olive tree that is God's historical people (Rom 11:11–24). Gentiles became part of God's people through circumcision of the heart (Rom 2:25–29), an experience expected by the prophet Jeremiah and the tradition found in Deuteronomy (Jer 4:4; 9:25–26; Deut 30:6; cf. Jer 31:31–34). It was now available through the gift of the Spirit as part of the promise associated with the coming of the Messiah. The conversion and inclusion of the Gentiles meant that the time promised by the prophets— when the Gentiles would worship the one true God—had arrived. Wherever and however the world or the church divides humanity into first-class and second-class people by virtue of their race or ethnicity or gender, Paul issues a call to reconciliation and inclusion through Christ (see Romans 14–15; Galatians [esp. 3:28]; Ephesians 2–3; Col 3:11).

Some try to turn Paul's conversion and resulting inclusive gospel into a gospel that is so inclusive as to exclude no one. This, however, betrays Paul's conversion experience and gospel. The inclusion that Paul experiences, preaches, and practices is not an inclusion lacking teeth or limits. His gospel does not say, "All are welcome just as they are," but rather, "All are welcome just as they are to be apprehended by, and fully converted to, Jesus Christ the Lord." The implications of that for *all* people will be explored later. For now, we may simply say that Paul's conversion leads him to value diversity of gender, ethnicity, and socio-economic status (Gal 3:28). And because of his historical and personal context, his conversion especially steers him away from nationalism and ethnocentrism, and toward what we call multiculturalism.

Summary

The Paul we have encountered in this chapter is someone who will provoke us, especially if we are attuned to the violence, exclusion, and empire that mark our contemporary situation. But Paul's critique of these realities, together with his corollary commitments to nonviolence, inclusion, and reconciliation, are not commitments to abstract principles. Rather, they are commitments that derive from his fundamental commitment to a person, the resurrected Jesus whom he encountered as God's envoy, Messiah, and Son. Arrested by this Jesus, Paul sought from then on to be conformed to him, the image of God himself (2 Cor 3:12—4:4, esp. 3:18). As we will see in later chapters, this conformity to Jesus the Messiah is not human effort at imitation; it is surrender to a transforming power that surrounded and infused Paul, as well as the communities he founded.

Paul's goal as an evangelist and pastor was to call others to the same Jesus and thus the same experience of God. He did, and still does, this through his preaching, example, and letter-writing. And, like Dr. King, with whom we began this chapter, Paul paid dearly for his work. We will examine these aspects of the apostle in the next chapter.

Reflection

1. How can our understanding of conversion and call be enlarged by the story of Saul/Paul being apprehended and sent by God in Christ?

2. Why is opposition to empire, along with practices of peacemaking/nonviolence and racial/ethnic inclusion and equality, central to a fully Christian understanding of conversion? How do nonviolence and inclusion/equality relate also to a fully Christian understanding of call and mission?

3. What "empires" might Paul critique today?

4. For Christians, are there ever limits—perhaps especially limits that Paul might not have anticipated—either to nonviolence or to racial/ethnic inclusion?

"To Spread the Gospel"

Missionary, Pastor, Letter-Writer

✣ Paul was an apostle, an ambassador—a missionary, we might say (though Paul himself does not know that word). For many people the word "missionary" conjures up images of people from colonial powers imposing their beliefs on less powerful people, whose cultures they were, or are, also intent on converting—or destroying. Such "missionaries" have sometimes even solicited their homeland's military forces to further their causes.

This is *not* what we mean when we call Paul a missionary. Rather, Paul believed himself to be caught up in a divine mission—a mission not everyone appreciated—to spread a powerful word of good news (the "gospel")[1] that would establish an international network of transformed, peaceable, multicultural communities worshipping and obeying the one true God by conformity to his Son in the power of the Spirit.[2] Paul subsequently fortified those communities by paying visits and writing letters.

1. The word "gospel" means "good news"; the next chapter contains a summary of the content of this good news.

2. "Conformity" as Paul understands it is not something rigid or robotic but creative, referring to a similar life-pattern, sometimes called "non-identical repetition."

Paul's Missionary and Pastoral Ministry

Acts correctly creates the impression that Paul was an itinerant preacher and community builder who constantly nourished the communities he founded. But Acts says nothing of Paul's rather prolific career as a letter writer. His letters, however, confirm the impression created by Acts that Paul traveled a lot, founded numerous "Jesus-communities," and cared for them in profound and practical ways, both during and after his founding of each of them.

Traveling in the ancient world was not uncommon, but neither was it easy, fast, or cheap. Acts depicts a series of three "missionary trips," into which at least some of Paul's letters can be fitted, and during which Paul may have logged some 10,000 miles. He probably walked the miles he did not sail, and though Roman roads were good, they sometimes passed through the mountainous terrain of what is now modern Turkey and Greece, the areas in which Paul spent the majority of his time. Traveling was thus an expense and a challenge, one exacerbated by human impediments, like roadside thieves, and natural impediments, like storms at sea. Paul experienced them all.

But not alone. The image of Paul as a "lone-ranger" missionary is simply false. He had traveling companions, emissaries, secretaries, co-authors for his letters, fellow political troublemakers (who then sometimes became fellow prisoners!), and other colleagues, including a husband-wife team, Prisca/Priscilla and Aquila, who were fellow tentmakers as well as gospel-workers.[3] Paul's tentmaking skills permitted him to support his travels and preaching with his own hands—some-

3. Acts 18:2–3, 18, 26; Rom 16:3; 1 Cor 16:19; 2 Tim 4:19.

thing he saw as an integral part of his ministry and as part of his correlation with the story of a self-emptying Messiah (1 Corinthians 9; Phil 2:6–11), but which others apparently saw as demeaning the message. Although Paul did not have a huge entourage like some rock star or popular political figure, his ability to work "night and day" (1 Thess 2:9; 2 Thess 3:8) allowed him to preach with integrity and still provide for himself and a few colleagues. Only after he established a community would he accept money from it, not as payment for services, but as a means for the community to participate in the work of God, either by supporting Paul directly (Phil 4:10–19) or by supporting his collection from largely Gentile churches for the poor Jewish believers in Jerusalem (Rom 15:22–29; 1 Cor 16:1–4; 2 Cor 8–9).

As an evangelist and community architect, Paul was a strategic thinker. For one thing, he targeted large, urban, cosmopolitan areas, where some converts could take the gospel with them either into more rural areas or on to the next city. As an urban missionary, Paul encountered all the challenges of an ancient city, including its larger religious, theopolitical, and economic dimensions, which his gospel sometimes confronted in public ways, as well as the differences among various people that make community life challenging.

Another aspect of Paul's strategy, according to Acts, was to make his way into a city through its Jewish community, from which he hoped to establish a core group of believers in Jesus as the Messiah. Some of his synagogue success was likely due to the presence and openness of "godfearers." These were Gentiles who associated with Jewish communities, attracted by Jewish monotheism and morality, without becoming full-fledged Jews. After efforts in the Jewish community succeeded, usually in a limited way, or failed, Paul moved on to Gentiles. Gentiles, including godfearers, constituted the majority of his converts.

The small communities of believers in Jesus as Messiah and Lord were called "assemblies," the Greek word *ekklēsia* meaning originally the assembly of a city's (or a civic group's) leaders for discussion and decision making. A Pauline *ekklēsia* was thus an *alternative* assembly (see further in chapter 10), a political or civic body with a different agenda—allegiance to the lordship of Jesus. Such an *ekklēsia* would meet in someone's house (Rom 16:5; 1 Cor 16:19; Col 4:15; Phlm 1:2), a residence as small as a tenement apartment or as large as a villa. Those who assembled constituted a new kind of family, calling themselves "brothers [and sisters]." Paul was their earthly spiritual father and mother, the one who nurtured and disciplined the children (1 Thess 2:1–12; 1 Cor 4:14–21), with God as the heavenly Father of all (Rom 8:15). Paul sometimes exercised his parental responsibilities in person and sometimes by proxy, in the form of personal ambassadors, such as Timothy and Titus, or letters. Today we would call a person like Paul a "pastor" (meaning "shepherd"), and his or her letters "pastoral letters."

Persecution and Suffering

The picture we have sketched thus far might suggest that Paul's ministry was one huge success story. As noted earlier, however, Paul frequently encountered opposition—sometimes even from fellow Jesus-followers and self-styled apostles. The suffering that resulted became a badge of honor for Paul because it expressed identification with the crucified Jesus.

Paul catalogs these sufferings on several occasions, including the following fairly comprehensive list in 2 Corinthians:

> [23]Are they [Paul's opponents] ministers of Christ? I am talking like a madman—I am a better one: with far greater labors, far more imprisonments, with countless floggings, and often near death. [24]Five times I have received from the Jews the forty lashes minus one. [25]Three times I was beaten with rods. Once I received a stoning. Three times I was shipwrecked; for a night and a day I was adrift at sea; [26]on frequent journeys, in danger from rivers, danger from bandits, danger from my own people, danger from Gentiles, danger in the city, danger in the wilderness, danger at sea, danger from false brothers and sisters; [27]in toil and hardship, through many a sleepless night, hungry and thirsty, often without food, cold and naked. [28]And, besides other things, I am under daily pressure because of my anxiety for all the churches. (2 Cor 11:23–28)[4]

The variety of trials depicted here is quite astounding: political imprisonment and torture, hellish travel experiences, dangers in areas both urban and remote, physical deprivation, mental stress, and more.

Does this text indicate that Paul was a masochist, and an arrogant one as well? No. Paul did not seek suffering or find it pleasurable (see 2 Cor 1:3–11). Rather, this kind of suffering was—and is still today—the result of radical faithfulness. It is, sometimes, the inevitable consequence of being conformed to a *crucified* Lord. As 2 Timothy puts it: "Indeed, all who want

4. See also additional lists in Rom 8:35; 1 Cor 4:8–13; 2 Cor 1:3–11; 4:7–12; 6:3–10; 12:10; plus general statements in Phil 1:29–30 and Col 1:24, among others.

to live a godly life in Christ Jesus will be persecuted" (3:12). Paul's apparent arrogance sounds, by his own admission (verse 23 above), deranged. It is a reversal of Roman values and a rhetorical device intended to challenge claims to apostleship that is not accompanied by adversity. Paul thereby implicitly describes faithful Christian witness as marked by the sign of the cross, an interpretation all but lost today in an age of "health and wealth" gospels and of mega-churches that specialize in marketing to "customers." For Paul, however, suffering, especially apostolic suffering, could ironically lead to the growth of the gospel (Philippians 1).[5]

It is true, however, that Paul's faithful suffering is the key to his "self-esteem," if not, as some would insist, arrogance. The word "apostle" is a title of authority. But what confirmed an apostolic call for Paul was not merely the claim of a divine encounter and commission—such claims are a dime a dozen—but above all conformity to Christ in his faithfulness, love, and (consequentially) suffering. This paradoxical reality of authority in suffering, or more generally of power in weakness (see 2 Cor 12:10: "whenever I am weak, then I am strong"), was for Paul the hallmark of apostleship. It authenticated him and authorized him to speak with the authority of God, whether in person or by letter.[6]

Letters: Apostleship by Proxy

Letters are a fascinating expression of the human spirit, of creativity and community. Their near-extinction—or their

5. For an insightful theological treatment of suffering in Paul's letters and contemporary experience, see Jervis, *At the Heart of the Gospel.*

6. Nonetheless, Paul distinguished his own inspired, authoritative voice from that of Jesus; see 1 Cor 7:10, 12, 25, 40.

transformation into email—may be one of the great losses of the digital age. Few things are more interesting to read than others' correspondence, especially if at least one of the parties is a gifted writer, like a C. S. Lewis. Plus there is the sense of tame voyeurism we experience when we peek over a person's shoulder to read someone else's mail.

As chapter 1 suggested, however, when we read Paul's letters, we are not really reading someone else's mail but letters directed to us, to all who share the faith of Paul's first letter-recipients. Those letters are *pastoral* letters, written by a spiritual father/mother to provide guidance for his children. They should therefore not be read as philosophical or theological discourses—though they are quite rhetorically sophisticated—but as documents of spiritual formation. Nonetheless, the letters are products of their time, and must also be read for what they are: first-century letters.

Reading a Letter from Paul

Ancient letters, like modern ones, had a fairly predictable format, which consisted of the following main parts:

Letter Part	Example from 1 Corinthians
Salutation ("X to Y, Greetings")	1:1–3/ [1]*Paul*, called to be an apostle of Christ Jesus by the will of God, *and* our brother *Sosthenes*, [2]*To the church of God that is in Corinth*, to those who are sanctified in Christ Jesus, called to be saints, together with all those who in every place call on the name of our Lord Jesus Christ, both their Lord and ours: [3]*Grace to you and peace* from God our Father and the Lord Jesus Christ.

Thanksgiving	1:4–9/ ⁴I give ***thanks*** to my God always for you because of the grace of God that has been given you in Christ Jesus. . . ⁷so that you are not lacking in any spiritual gift as you wait for the revealing of our Lord Jesus Christ. . . .
Body[a]	1:10—15:58/ 1¹⁰***Now I appeal to you***, brothers and sisters, by the name of our Lord Jesus Christ, that all of you be in agreement and that there be no divisions among you, but that you be united in the same mind and the same purpose. . . . 15⁵⁸***Therefore***, my beloved, be steadfast, immovable, always excelling in the work of the Lord, because you know that in the Lord your labor is not in vain.
Closing Exhortations[b]	16:1–18/ ¹Now concerning the collection for the saints: ***you should follow the directions I gave*** to the churches of Galatia. . . . ¹³***Keep alert, stand firm in your faith, be courageous, be strong.*** ¹⁴***Let all that you do be done in love.*** . . . ¹⁶***I urge you*** to put yourselves at the service of such people, and of everyone who works and toils with them. . . .
Greetings, benediction, etc.	16:19–24/ ¹⁹The churches of Asia send ***greetings.*** . . . ²⁰. . . ***Greet one another*** with a holy kiss. ²¹***I, Paul, write this greeting*** with my own hand. . . . ²³The ***grace*** of the Lord Jesus be with you. ²⁴My ***love*** be with all of you in Christ Jesus.

[a] The letter body will of course vary in length; in 1 Corinthians it is quite long and covers an array of subjects. The contents include argument, example, exhortation, etc.

[b] These final words sometimes include travel plans.

It is helpful to be aware of these parts when reading the letters. Paul "christianizes" the various elements of the letter to adapt them to his purposes. For example, Paul's salutations provide important theological descriptions of the parties involved. He takes the standard ancient letter greeting, "hello" (Greek *chairein*), and converts it to "grace [*charis*] and peace"—a creative play on words rooted in the Scriptures and the gospel. The thanksgiving often has a potent rhetorical function in Paul's letters; it may, for instance, develop into a short summary of the letter's theme (as in 1 Cor 1:4–9).[7] And the letter's final words have deep pastoral and spiritual import.

Throughout each letter, but especially in the body, Paul employs a large arsenal of rhetorical techniques borrowed from both Greco-Roman rhetoricians and Jewish rabbis. He tries to move hearts, shape minds, explain the truth of his gospel, defend his ministry, and form communal character. He does so by quoting and commenting on Scripture, drawing on Jesus' teaching and early Christian tradition, unpacking the significance of his basic beliefs and the churches' practices, and above all focusing attention on the first and second comings of Jesus: his past cross and resurrection and his future coming, or *parousia*. In other words, he presents his churches with a "bifocal" vision of Christ past and future, which permits them to understand Christ present, Christ here and now.[8]

7. In 1 Thessalonians the thanksgiving morphs into a long narrative (through 3:13) with a concluding prayer-wish, all of which expresses thanksgiving (see 3:9) for how God has preserved the Thessalonians through persecution. In Galatians, a stinging word of disappointment and anger replaces and parodies the thanksgiving (Gal 1:6–10).

8. For more on the notion of "bifocal" vision and existence in Christ, see chapters 5 and 11.

An Overview of the Letters

There are thirteen letters in the New Testament bearing Paul's name, as well as one anonymous document—the Letter to the Hebrews—that, over the centuries, many have mistakenly thought to be Paul's work. The letters ascribed to Paul, in the order in which they now appear in the Christian Bible, are:

- Romans
- 1 and 2 Corinthians
- Galatians
- Ephesians
- Philippians
- Colossians
- 1 and 2 Thessalonians
- 1 and 2 Timothy
- Titus
- Philemon

These letters are organized into two main groups, letters to churches (Romans—2 Thessalonians) and letters to individuals (1 Timothy—Philemon). Within each group they appear in order, approximately, of their length, from longest to shortest.

Due to differences in style, content, and historical allusions, six of these thirteen documents are disputed as to their actual authorship by Paul: Ephesians, Colossians, 2 Thessalonians, 1 and 2 Timothy, and Titus. While it is possible that some or all of these were written by disciples of Paul in his name after his death, it is also quite likely that some of the differences among the letters are due to the frequently underestimated role of Paul's colleagues and assistants, who served as co-authors, secretaries, and bearers/interpreters for the letters.[9] When we read the New Testament, including Paul's letters, as *Scripture*, we want to learn as much as we can about who wrote the various documents (including when, why, and how), but often we cannot know as much as we would like. It is important to recognize that the inspiration of a Scriptural text is not dependent on its authorship—or on our knowledge of its author.[10]

The themes of the various Pauline letters are summarized in the following table:[11]

9. In my view, the only two letters that may not bear the more-or-less direct mark of the apostle are 1 Timothy and Titus. In the chapters that follow, we shall draw largely on the undisputed letters in analyzing Paul's message, with backup from some of the disputed documents.

10. Some people are understandably uncomfortable with the possibility of New Testament letters being penned in the name of an apostle by a later writer, for that phenomenon (called "pseudonymity") appears fraudulent. We should not, however, impose contemporary understandings of either authorship or honesty on ancient texts. Furthermore, if (and I stress if) the New Testament contains examples of the ancient custom of honoring great teachers by (a) adapting their ideas for a later generation and (b) writing in the teacher's name, there is no theological reason to think that such texts are uninspired. A healthy understanding of inspiration includes a recognition of all the human factors that go into the production of a document that later becomes recognized as Scripture.

11. These summary phrases are adapted from those used in Gorman, *Apostle*.

Letter	Approximate Date	Theme
Romans	late 50s	Gentile and Jew in cruciform covenant community: the goal of the gospel
1 Corinthians	mid-50s	chaos and the cross in Corinth: the subversion of the status quo
2 Corinthians	mid-50s	Paul's defense of cruciform ministry: the way of reconciliation
Galatians	early to mid-50s	the sufficiency of the cross and Spirit: the fulfillment of the covenant and the promises
Ephesians	60s (or later?)	walking worthily of the cosmic crucified Christ: a community of grace, reconciliation, and love
Philippians	mid-late 50s	the hymn of the crucified Lord in the cruciform community: God's politics in daily life
Colossians	early 60s?	the cosmic crucified Christ as the wisdom of God: the fullness of God and the fullness of life

1 Thessalonians	late 40s or very early 50s	holiness and hope in a pagan world: the essentials of faith, love, and hope
2 Thessalonians	early 50s (or later)	cruciform faithfulness and goodness before the *parousia*: God's judgment and human responsibility
1 Timothy	after Paul's death?	proper order and conduct in God's household: structures and ministries for the people of God
2 Timothy	early 60s?	suffering rather than shame: fighting the good fight
Titus	after Paul's death?	ordering church life and leadership between Christ's epiphanies: salvation and church polity
Philemon	50s	the cross and the structures of this world: the slave is my brother

It will be useful to consider the content of each of these letters, at least briefly, in canonical order.

Romans is Paul's longest and most famous letter, written in the late fifties to house churches in the capital of the empire, which Paul had not yet visited. Paul writes to them in part to introduce himself and his gospel, perhaps in order to garner their financial support for his planned mission trip to Spain. Often thought to be a theological treatise, Romans does indeed contain Paul's most systematic presentation of his gospel, but it is still a real, pastoral letter. Paul seeks to bring together Gentile and Jewish believers by explaining his gospel in detail. He reminds them of the universal reality of sin and the corresponding need for reconciliation with God, which God in faithfulness to the covenant with Israel has graciously and lovingly brought about through the faithful and loving death of his Son. To this grace Gentiles and Jews alike are summoned to respond in faith by dying with Christ and rising to new life with him in baptism, beginning a new life of faith/obedience, love, and hope. Paul's goal is to form a cross-shaped (cruciform) community that practices tolerance of cultural differences within the community while extending grace and hospitality toward outsiders.

The Corinthian correspondence, *1 and 2 Corinthians*, is part of an exchange of letters between Paul and the community of house churches he had founded in the important Roman colony of Corinth in southern Greece. Corinth had become Paul's base of operations for that part of Greece, and he apparently wrote more frequently to the churches there than anywhere else, though only these two documents remain intact. The two letters date from the mid-fifties and reveal a community often in turmoil, not least of all because of their relationship with Paul!

1 Corinthians, which is actually at least the second letter Paul sent to Corinth,[12] is Paul's attempt to deal with a series of interrelated issues in the house churches: divisions and misunderstanding about ministers, sexual immorality and confusion, litigation among believers, controversy about eating meat offered to idols, problems surrounding the Lord's

12. Paul refers to a letter before our 1 Corinthians (1 Cor 5:9) and another one before our 2 Corinthians (2 Cor 7:8).

supper and worship, and misunderstandings about the general resurrection. Paul offers a unified pastoral and theological vision of life together as the body of Christ that embodies the upside-down, counter-imperial values of Christ crucified, resurrected, and coming. Such a life looks out, in love, for the needs of others, especially the weak, and treats both the church body and the human body as the sphere of Christ's holy presence.

2 Corinthians, which is at least Paul's fourth letter to Corinth, tackles head-on another series of interrelated problems involving Paul's relationship to the community. The letter unfolds in three parts. Part one (chapters 1–7) focuses on Paul's attempt to reconcile with the Corinthians. Part two (chapters 8–9) is a theologically rich appeal, based on God's grace in Christ, for the Corinthians to generously support Paul's collection for the Jerusalem church. Part three (chapters 10–13) is Paul's polemical attack on teachers he calls "false" and (sarcastically) "super" apostles, who oppose Paul and, according to him, embody and preach a false gospel. Paul counters with a defense of his own Christlike ministry, characterized by weakness and suffering.

Galatians is a letter with one concern: whether Gentiles need to become law-observant Jews as well as "Christians" in order to be full members of God's covenant people. The presenting issue is the demand made by some teachers in Galatia, part of what is now central Turkey, that Gentile men who have received the Spirit and have been baptized into Christ must also be circumcised. Paul answers angrily with a resounding "no," arguing that those who have been crucified with Christ in faith and baptism, and are thus in Christ, have become heirs of the promises to Abraham and his (one) "seed," or "offspring"—Christ—and are thus adopted children of God. The proof of this is their possession of the Spirit, who guides them in a fruitful life of faith, hope, and love to fulfill the "law of Christ."

Ephesians, though disputed with respect to authorship and probably indebted to Colossians for some of its content, is a carefully structured document. The first half contains theology that serves as the basis for the ethics contained in the second half. Ephesians presents a cosmic Christ in whom the church, which is richly blessed in Christ, dwells as a community of Gentiles and Jews who are saved by grace and reconciled to one another. They exist as one body with different gifts, but with a common ethic of compassion, respect, and holiness that is expressed in mutual relations both within the church itself and within the Christian household.

Philippians is one of Paul's "prison letters," written while Paul was somewhere in jail to the church in Philippi, a leading city of the province of Macedonia in northern Greece. The letter, which contains several important political images, is an extended commentary on its central text, 2:6–11. This text is a poem that celebrates Christ's self-humbling, self-emptying incarnation and death, followed by God's exaltation of him to the position of Lord. The first half of the poem is described as the "mind" or disposition of Christ, serving as an example of love and humility in the service of unity. Paul himself and others are described as human exemplars of this mind of Christ. Those who have this Christ-disposition experience inexplicable peace and joy, even when suffering, and anticipate a future share in Christ's resurrection.

Colossians is a disputed prison letter addressed to a community in what is now western Turkey. The church is confronting an apparently syncretistic "philosophy" that appears to combine Jewish food practices, mysticism, and asceticism as the way to wisdom and God. The letter's response to this is to highlight Christ as the fullness of divinity and wisdom, and to describe life in Christ as resurrection with him to a seat above all cosmic powers, which have in fact been defeated by Christ on the cross. Daily life is still firmly planted in this world, however, and is characterized by love, purity, peace, and joy.

1 and 2 Thessalonians are addressed to a community of believers in the important Macedonian city of Thessaloniki, a port in northern Greece. *1 Thessalonians*, probably Paul's earliest surviving letter, reveals much about the suffering (from persecution) of the Thessalonians and of Paul, Paul's ministry, and the relationship between Paul and the church. It contains exhortations to faithfulness, love, and peace, with special emphasis on the imminent *parousia* ("second coming," or "royal appearance") of Jesus as the basis of both hope and holiness. *2 Thessalonians* is one of the disputed letters, partly because it provides, in contrast to 1 Thessalonians, an outline of certain events that must occur before the return of the Lord.

1 and 2 Timothy and Titus as a group are generally called the Pastoral Epistles because they are addressed to Paul's younger colleagues who have pastoral, or ministerial, responsibilities. All three are disputed letters and considered by many scholars to have been written after Paul's death by one of his "disciples," though some see 2 Timothy as more authentic, perhaps containing fragments of Paul's own work. *1 Timothy* and *Titus* focus on the qualifications and responsibilities of various kinds of church leaders (deacon, elder/presbyter, etc.). There are also guidelines for other aspects of church life, and both letters preserve important early Christian creedal and hymnic fragments. *2 Timothy* is a much more personal letter, encouraging Timothy to be willing to suffer shame and persecution for the gospel, as the faithful Paul himself has done.

Philemon is a very brief prison letter to a Christian slave owner, converted by Paul, named Philemon, and to the church in his house. It encourages Philemon to accept his slave Onesimus, also converted by Paul—during this imprisonment—as a brother and, it appears, even to release him.

Summary

The letters Paul wrote were expressions of his ministry of forming communities of Gentiles and Jews dedicated to Jesus as God's Messiah and Lord. In the thirteen letters ascribed to him, we find the apostle consoling and cajoling, arguing and expounding, reasoning and pleading. We find him "theologizing"—but only as a means of pastoral or spiritual direction. Many of the issues he addresses are still our issues, and his perspectives are no less provocative—or relevant—today.

One way for us to proceed at this point would be to examine each letter in more detail, but we will pursue another route. From the letters of Paul emerge a set of what we might call "Paul's big ideas." Following an overview of Paul's gospel, we will examine eight of these Pauline essentials.

Reflection

1. How might the shape of Paul's ministry serve as a paradigm of ministry today?

2. What is the role of suffering in the growth of the gospel, Christian communities, and individual Christians today?

3. What is the significance of the fact that Paul's theology comes to us in the form of pastoral correspondence?

4. How do you understand inspiration? How does this understanding affect your reaction to the discussion about authorship?

4

"The Power of God for Salvation"

An Overview of Paul's Gospel

✣ The term "evangelist" is sometimes no more popular, and no less misunderstood, than "missionary," which we looked at in chapter 3. "Evangelist" is often associated with television preachers and "crusade" leaders like Billy Graham. Paul was an evangelist—a preacher of the evangel (Greek *euangelion*), or good news—but not in the narrow sense of someone seeking individual converts through rather anonymous activity. Paul, as we have stressed, was not just an itinerant preacher, but also a pastor. He was, nevertheless, a preacher—a proclaimer of the good news of God's intervention in human history through Jesus Christ. This good news was not a private message of personal salvation, though it included the salvation of individuals. It was a *political* announcement, or better a *theopolitical* announcement (politics involving God), that challenged—and challenges—the very core of how people relate to one another in the real world.[1]

Many in the modern or postmodern world claim, contrary to their actual experiences, that religion or spirituality

1. By "political" I do not primarily mean government structures and political parties but rather the more fundamental reality of a public, common life together. The "body politic" relates on a variety of levels, both within itself and toward other political bodies, and the good news it embodies challenges every dimension of life together.

41

and politics can and should be separated. Religion is supposedly personal and private, while politics is obviously public. That this divorce of religion from politics does not exist and does not work is clear from the daily news. The ancients did not try to mask the connection. They saw God or the gods as deeply interested in human affairs; so too with Jesus and then Paul. Jesus was not crucified for preaching a search for God within, as the noncanonical Gospel of Thomas describes his message, but for preaching the coming of the reign of God, a political image that stirred up both hope among Jews and fear among Romans. Paul was no different; he preached the "gospel" of God.

Paul did not leave us with one comprehensive statement of his gospel, much less his entire teaching, or theology. But he did leave some very important summaries that will provide the major framework for eight essentials, or "big ideas," to be presented in the chapters following this overview. It is crucial to note, however, that these "big ideas" are not abstract beliefs or even deeply held convictions that stay in the head; they are important aspects of Paul's spirituality (lived experience of God) and of the spirituality he sought to nurture among the communities that heard or read, and continue to hear or read, his letters.

"Gospel" in Context

First-century people who heard the Greek word *euangelion* associated the term with the good news of God's salvation as foretold by the prophets (if they knew the Jewish Scriptures), especially Isaiah, and/or with the good news of the emperor's birth, accession to power, or "salvation" that he offered to all.

We see this in three famous texts, two from Isaiah and one from an inscription, dated about 9 BC, found in Priene, near Ephesus (located in the Western part of modern Turkey).

> [7]How beautiful upon the mountains are the feet of the messenger who announces peace [*euange-lizomenou akoēn eirēnēs*], who brings good news [*euangelizomenos agatha*], who announces salvation, who says to Zion, "Your God reigns." [8]Listen! Your sentinels lift up their voices, together they sing for joy; for in plain sight they see the return of the LORD to Zion. [9]Break forth together into singing, you ruins of Jerusalem; for the LORD has comforted his people, he has redeemed Jerusalem. [10]The LORD has bared his holy arm before the eyes of all the nations; and all the ends of the earth shall see the salvation of our God. (Isa 52:7–10)

> [1]The spirit of the Lord GOD is upon me, because the LORD has anointed me; he has sent me to bring good news [*euangelisasthai*] to the oppressed, to bind up the brokenhearted, [2]to proclaim liberty to the captives, and release to the prisoners; to proclaim the year of the Lord's favor, and the day of vengeance of our God; to comfort all who mourn. (Isa 61:1–2)

> The providence which has ordered the whole of our life, showing concern and zeal, has ordained the most perfect consummation for human life by giving to it Augustus, by filling him with virtue for doing the work of a benefactor among men, and by sending in him, as it were, a savior for us and those who come after us, to make war to cease, to create

> order everywhere. . . [S]ince the Caesar [Augustus] through his appearance has exceeded the hopes of all former good messages [*euangelia*], surpassing not only the benefactors who came before him, but also leaving no hope that anyone in the future would surpass him, and since for the world the birthday of the god was the beginning of his good messages [*euangelia*]. . . . (Priene inscription)

When Paul preached the gospel of God, he was announcing that what Isaiah had predicted was being *fulfilled*, and what the inscription at Priene proclaimed was being *challenged*. God's politics were about to replace Caesar's. As the prominent biblical scholar N. T. Wright says, if Jesus is Lord, Caesar is not. The Priene inscription calls Caesar "savior"—savior of the world, bringer of peace and justice—to which Paul says, "No way!" We must add, therefore, that if God is savior, Caesar is not. And if God's salvation, including peace and justice, comes through Jesus, then it does *not* come through Caesar—or any other political or imperial force or figure.

This does not mean that Paul's gospel was political *rather than* religious; it is just that the two were inseparable. Words like justice (or righteousness), salvation, savior, peace, church (or assembly), gospel and, of course, Christ (Messiah) were—and are—both political *and* religious because they had to do with how people relate to both God and others in the real world. Paul's gospel, therefore, is *theopolitical*.

According to Paul, *the gospel of God is not a set of propositions; it is the account of the planned, executed, and soon-to-be-consummated benevolent intervention of God into the history of Israel, human history more generally, and the entire cosmos to set right a world gone awry.* Both the intervention itself and the retelling of it effect transformation in those who receive the message for what it is—good news of God's action in Christ and the Spirit. This is why the gospel is "the power of God for salvation to everyone who has faith, to the Jew first and also to the Greek" (Rom 1:16).

Because the gospel is about God's dramatic, cosmic, benevolent intervention, it is not merely a message about personal salvation, as so many perversions of the gospel imply. To be sure, Paul's gospel calls individuals to a right relationship with God, but it calls them into a community where right relationships with God and with others—both insiders and outsiders—are taught, learned, and practiced. Those who believe Paul's gospel are not first and foremost invited to eternal life when they die (though that is included: Rom 5:21; 6:22–23), but to a new life in this world under the sway of a new lord and savior in the company of like-minded companions (Phil 1:27—2:16).[2] Hence the adjective "theopolitical" to describe the gospel, meaning a narrative about God that creates a public life together, a corporate narrative, that is an alternative to the status quo in the Roman Empire, the American empire, or any other body politic.

The Gospel Proclaimed

The gospel Paul preached, then, is good news—good news *from* God, *about* his Son, and *for* us. These elements are overlapping and inseparable (see, e.g., Rom 1:1–17; 3:21–26). The gospel is a powerful force unleashed in the world that accomplishes its purpose of salvation, or rescue and transfor-

2. The Greek of Phil 1:27 contains a play on words that might best be rendered "Let your body politic be worthy of the gospel of Christ. . . ."

mation (Rom 1:16–17). It is a power because it is a word from God, and whenever God's voice sounds forth, something incredible happens—like creation (Genesis 1) or salvation (Isa 55:10–11).

As a "word" from God, the good news is obviously not a single word but a narrative account of God's activity in Christ. As we will see below, this narrative can be expressed in a variety of ways, but it centers on Jesus' death, resurrection, and exaltation as Lord. Although this narrative is inherently powerful, its proclamation makes a claim on listeners that requires a human response to this great and gracious divine initiative: the gospel is the power of God for "everyone who has faith" (Rom 1:16). Paul refers to this response, then, as "having faith" or "believing" (Greek *pistis/pisteuō*), but we must be careful not to take a minimalist view of this word. As we will see in several subsequent chapters, "faith" is a rich, robust term that indicates a full intellectual, emotional, volitional, and behavioral response to what God has done.

When Paul actually evangelized, he would have had ample time to explain this good news in some detail. In his letters he offers relatively brief narrative accounts of the gospel, which he then unpacks throughout those letters, demonstrating the way of life appropriate to those who believe this good news. Paul likely inherited some of these narrative accounts, which are like mini-creeds or confessions of faith, from already existing communities of Christ-followers. Others he probably composed himself. We list some of both here, following the NRSV and presented, after the first text, in canonical order:

a. The following very short confession of faith, with wide-ranging theopolitical and existential implications, was probably very common in the early churches (see chapter 8):

> *Romans 10:9; 1 Corinthians 12:3; Philippians 2:11:*
> "Jesus [Christ] is Lord."

b. This brief summary, with echoes of earlier Christian tradition, stresses the gospel's continuity with the Scriptures of Israel:

> *Romans 1:1–4:* [1] . . . the gospel of God, [2]which he promised beforehand through his prophets in the holy scriptures, [3]the gospel concerning his Son, who was descended from David according to the flesh [4]and was declared to be Son of God with power according to the spirit of holiness by resurrection from the dead, Jesus Christ our Lord. . . .

c. The following dense text again has echoes of pre-Pauline tradition and again emphasizes continuity with the Scriptures as well as the gracious initiative of God in the saving death of Jesus:

> *Romans 3:21–26:* [21]But now, apart from law, the righteousness of God has been disclosed, and is attested by the law and the prophets, [22]the righteousness of God through the faith of [or, "faith in"] Jesus Christ for all who believe. For there is no distinction, [23]since all have sinned and fall short of the glory of God; [24]they are now justified by his grace as a gift, through the redemption that is in Christ Jesus, [25]whom God put forward as a sacrifice of atonement by his blood, effective through faith.

He did this to show his righteousness, because in his divine forbearance he had passed over the sins previously committed; [26]it was to prove at the present time that he himself is righteous and that he justifies the one who shares the faith of [or, "has faith in"] Jesus.[3]

d. The next text appears to be Paul's own interpretation of the meaning of an early Christian creed (see 1 Cor 15:3–8 below), focusing on the participation of believers in Christ's death, burial, and resurrection:

Romans 6:3–11: [3]Do you not know that all of us who have been baptized into Christ Jesus were baptized into his death? [4]Therefore we have been buried with him by baptism into death, so that, just as Christ was raised from the dead by the glory of the Father, so we too might walk in newness of life. [5]For if we have been united with him in a death like his, we will certainly be united with him in a resurrection like his. [6]We know that our old self was crucified with him so that the body of sin might be destroyed, and we might no longer be enslaved to sin. [7]For whoever has died is freed from sin. [8]But if we have died with Christ, we believe that we will also live with him. [9]We know that Christ, being raised from the dead, will never die again; death no longer has

3. Here I depart from the NRSV. In footnotes, the NRSV offers two alternative phrases about the "faith of" Jesus (meaning his faithfulness), one in v. 22 and one in v. 26, for the phrase "faith in Jesus/Jesus Christ." I have placed the two alternative phrases in the text itself and placed the original NRSV text in brackets. This change reflects the view of many scholars that the NRSV's alternative phrases better convey Paul's meaning. See also Gal 2:15–21 below.

dominion over him. ¹⁰The death he died, he died
to sin, once for all; but the life he lives, he lives to
God. ¹¹So you also must consider yourselves dead
to sin and alive to God in Christ Jesus.

e. This final excerpt from Romans, exhibiting Paul's own approach to scriptural interpretation, highlights the universality of the gospel and two of its most fundamental dimensions: Jesus' resurrection and lordship:

> *Romans 10:8–13*: ⁸But what does it [the Scripture]
> say? "The word is near you, on your lips and in your
> heart" (that is, the word of faith that we proclaim);
> ⁹because if you confess with your lips that Jesus is
> Lord and believe in your heart that God raised him
> from the dead, you will be saved. ¹⁰For one believes
> with the heart and so is justified, and one confesses
> with the mouth and so is saved. ¹¹The scripture
> says, "No one who believes in him will be put to
> shame." ¹²For there is no distinction between Jew
> and Greek; the same Lord is Lord of all and is gen-
> erous to all who call on him. ¹³For, "Everyone who
> calls on the name of the Lord shall be saved."

f. This quintessentially Pauline passage focuses on the crucified Messiah as God's counterintuitive wisdom and power:

> *1 Corinthians 1:18–25*: ¹⁸For the message about the
> cross is foolishness to those who are perishing, but
> to us who are being saved it is the power of God. . . .
> ²²For Jews demand signs and Greeks desire wisdom,
> ²³but we proclaim Christ crucified, a stumbling
> block to Jews and foolishness to Gentiles, ²⁴but
> to those who are the called, both Jews and Greeks,

Christ [crucified[4]] the power of God and the wisdom of God. [25]For God's foolishness is wiser than human wisdom, and God's weakness is stronger than human strength.

g. The next selection bears the marks of a fairly formal early creed, the "good news" (1 Cor 15:1) that Paul received and passed on, which recounts four key narrative moments in the gospel: Christ's death, burial, resurrection, and appearances:

1 Corinthians 15:3–8: [3]For I handed on to you as of first importance what I in turn had received: that Christ died for our sins in accordance with the scriptures, [4]and that he was buried, and that he was raised on the third day in accordance with the scriptures, [5]and that he appeared to Cephas, then to the twelve. . . . [8]Last of all, as to one untimely born, he appeared also to me.

h. This rich text celebrates the heart of Paul's gospel: the reconciling love of God in Christ, and the powerful effects of that love:

2 Corinthians 5:14–21: [14]For the love of Christ urges us on, because we are convinced that one has died for all; therefore all have died. [15]And he died for all, so that those who live might live no longer for themselves, but for him who died and was raised for them. . . .[17]So if anyone is in Christ, there is a new creation: everything old has passed away; see, everything has become new! [18]All this is from God,

4. Although the word crucified is not in the text, it is implicit from the context (see v. 23).

who reconciled us to himself through Christ, and has given us the ministry of reconciliation; [19]that is, in Christ God was reconciling the world to himself, not counting their trespasses against them, and entrusting the message of reconciliation to us. [20]So we are ambassadors for Christ, since God is making his appeal through us; we entreat you on behalf of Christ, be reconciled to God. [21]For our sake he made him to be sin who knew no sin, so that in him we might become the righteousness of God.

i. The following brief summary speaks in traditional apocalyptic language about a new reality: the liberating effects of Jesus' death:[5]

> *Galatians 1:3–5*: [3]Grace to you and peace from God our Father and the Lord Jesus Christ, [4]who gave himself for our sins to set us free from the present evil age, according to the will of our God and Father, [5]to whom be the glory forever and ever. Amen.

j. The following rich passage declares God's initiative and Christ's faithfulness and love in effecting our "justification," while expressing it in the vivid image of death and resurrection—co-crucifixion with Christ and new life to God by virtue of Christ living within:

> *Galatians 2:15–21*: [15]We ourselves are Jews by birth and not Gentile sinners; [16]yet we know that a person is justified not by the works of the law but through

---

5. The term "apocalyptic," discussed in the next chapter, refers to thought and language about the end of this evil age and the inbreaking of God's justice.

the faith of [or "faith in"] Jesus Christ. And we have come to believe in Christ Jesus, so that we might be justified by the faith of [or "faith in"] Christ, and not by doing the works of the law, because no one will be justified by the works of the law. . . . [19]For through the law I died to the law, so that I might live to God. I have been crucified with Christ; [20]and it is no longer I who live, but it is Christ who lives in me. And the life I now live in the flesh I live by the faith of [or "faith in"] the Son of God, who loved me and gave himself for me. [21]I do not nullify the grace of God; for if justification comes through the law, then Christ died for nothing. (NRSV, altered)

k. This text uses images of redemption and adoption, placed again within an apocalyptic framework highlighting God's time:

Galatians 4:4–5: [4]But when the fullness of time had come, God sent his Son, born of a woman, born under the law, [5]in order to redeem those who were under the law, so that we might receive adoption as children.

l. The following well-known text stresses God's mercy and grace while demonstrating the inseparability of good works from salvation:

Ephesians 2:4–10: [4]But God, who is rich in mercy, out of the great love with which he loved us [5]even when we were dead through our trespasses, made us alive together with Christ—by grace you have been saved—[6]and raised us up with him and seated us with him in the heavenly places in Christ Jesus. . . .

[8]For by grace you have been saved through faith, and this is not your own doing; it is the gift of God— [9]not the result of works, so that no one may boast. [10]For we are what he has made us, created in Christ Jesus for good works, which God prepared beforehand to be our way of life [or "that we might walk in them"].

m. Perhaps the most thoroughly studied and widely debated of all the summaries of Paul's gospel,[6] the following poetic text portrays Jesus' preexistent divine status, exemplary self-emptying incarnation and death, and exaltation to Lordship:

> *Philippians 2:5–11:* [5]Let the same mind be in you that was in Christ Jesus, [6]who, though he was in the form of God, did not regard equality with God as something to be exploited, [7]but emptied himself, taking the form of a slave, being born in human likeness. And being found in human form, [8]he humbled himself and became obedient to the point of death—even death on a cross. [9]Therefore God also highly exalted him and gave him the name that is above every name, [10]so that at the name of Jesus every knee should bend, in heaven and on earth and under the earth, [11]and every tongue should confess that Jesus Christ is Lord, to the glory of God the Father.

6. Many scholars believe this to be a pre-Pauline hymn adapted by Paul, but a growing number think Paul wrote it himself because it fits so well into the entire letter. In either case, since it is so central to his theology and its themes permeate his letters, we would not be wrong to call it his "master story."

n. This succinct gospel summary develops the theme of one-ness: one God, one humanity, one mediator:

> *1 Timothy 2:5–6*: [5]For there is one God; there is also one mediator between God and humankind, Christ Jesus, himself human, [6]who gave himself a ransom for all. . . .

o. Our final text recaps well-known themes while adding references to Jesus before Pontius Pilate and to his return ("manifestation"; Greek *epiphaneia*):

> *1 Timothy 6:13–15*: [13]In the presence of God, who gives life to all things, and of Christ Jesus, who in his testimony before Pontius Pilate made the good con-fession, I charge you [14]to keep the commandment without spot or blame until the manifestation of our Lord Jesus Christ, [15]which he will bring about at the right time—he who is the blessed and only Sovereign, the King of kings and Lord of lords.

Summary

Paul's gospel is a story of salvation for the human race in con-tinuity with Israel's Scriptures and in contrast to the gospel of Rome. In some respects, the variety in the way the story is recounted defies summary or synthesis, yet in many other respects clear themes emerge. From these and other key texts in the letters, we may identify eight "big ideas" in Paul:

- "In the Fullness of Time": Apocalyptic Crossroads
- "The Gospel of God": Covenant Faithfulness and Surprising Grace

- "Even Death on a Cross": The Meaning(s) of Christ's Death

- "God Raised" and "Highly Exalted Him": Jesus is Son of God and Lord

- "Justified by Faith . . . Crucified with Christ": Reconciliation with God through Participation in Christ

- "Called to be Saints": Countercultural, Multicultural Community in the Spirit

- "Conformed to the Image of God's Son": Cruciform Faith, Hope, and Love

- "The Glory about to be Revealed": Return, Resurrection, Renewal

A chapter will be devoted to each of these.

It should be noted in advance that anyone who tries to summarize Paul's gospel in eight words or phrases, even if they are Paul's own words (as here), is taking an enormous risk. Nevertheless, it will be helpful to those encountering Paul in a serious way, perhaps for the first time, to have a framework into which they may place what they read.[7]

Reflection

1. With what do you associate the term "gospel"? How is this association like and/or unlike that of Paul's first-century audience?

---

7. I am using the term "gospel" here and throughout this book to refer to Paul's message as a whole.

2. What strikes you as the "good news" in the various accounts of the gospel listed in this chapter?

3. How might the theopolitical and narrative (story-like, rather than merely propositional) character of Paul's gospel address our situation today?

5

"In the Fullness of Time"

Apocalyptic Crossroads

✤ One of the most important questions any spiritual tradition or leader can ask is "What time is it? Where are we in God's plan, or dream, for the human story?" Paul had an answer: the time was ripe, to borrow an image from gardening. Or, to use one from ancient timekeeping devices, as Paul did, the time was full (Gal 4:4).

Popular interpretations of Paul's phrase "in the fullness of time," referring to God's sending of the Son at just the right moment (Gal 4:4), often suggest that Paul had the time of the Roman Empire in mind. That is, the timing was perfect for the spread of the gospel—the existence of Roman roads, the use of a common language (Greek), and so on. Such phenomena certainly facilitated the spread of the gospel and the work of Paul. But the apostle has something more biblical, more Jewish in mind when he uses the phrase "the fullness of time." Paul is convinced that God has a plan for the world and for human history, a plan that unfolds as part of Israel's history and in a sequence best described in the language of prophets and apocalyptic seers—among whom Paul would place himself.

The words "apocalyptic" and "apocalypse" strike a chord of confusion or fear in the minds of many people. They imagine total chaos and destruction either in history, as in *Apocalypse Now*, the movie about the Vietnam War, or at the supposed end of history, as in the *Left Behind* series of books. But at the time of Jesus and Paul, apocalyptic thinking was commonplace, and Paul, like Jesus, had an apocalyptic perspective. Above all, this meant a conviction that the climax of the divine drama was at hand. This belief was rooted in the prophets of Israel.

Paul and the Apocalyptic Vision

In response to the idolatry and injustice, the violence and oppression, that the prophets witnessed, they spoke of something "new" that God was going to do, couching it in the language of the old—new creation, new exodus, new covenant. They imagined a future time of true worship that would include all the nations, an era of justice for Israel and for all, an age of peace and security, when the lion lies down with the lamb (Isa 11:1–9).

When this sort of vision failed to materialize in the course of historical events, the later prophets and their heirs, the apocalyptic visionaries, imagined a radical disjunction between the present age and the age to come, an abrupt transition from the one to the other prefaced by great upheavals in normal human life and even in the cosmos itself. Following these events, there would be a divine intervention to end the old and began the new. In anticipation of that day, the apocalyptic visionaries called the children of God to align themselves *now* with the one true God and the power of the age to come, over against the god of this age (Satan) and his minions (cosmic demons, political oppressors, and the like).

This thinking is called *dualistic*, because it sees everything in polarized dualities: this age versus the age to come, the god of this age versus the true God, the children of light versus the children of darkness, and so on. Such dualistic language was prominent among the breakaway Jews who moved into the desert near the Dead Sea and deposited their beliefs, written on scrolls, in caves for safekeeping. The apocalyptic vision of the Dead Sea Scrolls is at times quite violent; a messianic figure leads the sons of light into battle against the sons of darkness—the Roman oppressors.[1] The apocalyptic dimensions of the teaching of Jesus are to be found partially in his predictions of future cosmic events before the coming of the Son of Man (e.g., Mark 13). But more importantly, Jesus' apocalyptic perspective emerges in his central message: that the reign of God is breaking into history now—that is, in and through Jesus' own ministry of calling twelve to reconstitute Israel, preaching to the poor and to all, exorcising demons and defeating Satan, forgiving sins, liberating the oppressed, challenging the religious leaders, and eventually dying and rising.

For Paul, the event of Jesus Christ was God's perfectly timed means of effecting the transition from this age to the age to come, fulfilling the prophetic vision of something new and yet old: "If anyone is in Christ, there is a new creation!" (2 Cor 5:17). But Paul saw this apocalyptic event occurring in two parts—commonly referred to as the first and second comings of Christ—with an intervening era in which the two ages overlap (1 Cor 10:11) and during which period the

1. Similar images are found in Paul and especially Revelation, but human beings do not actually fight, and the language is therefore metaphorical.

present age is already beginning to pass away (1 Cor 7:31; cf. Rom 13:11–12). We may describe this framework, which is fundamental to understanding Paul, as follows:

Apocalyptic Intervention, Part I

- In the coming, death, resurrection, and exaltation of Jesus in the fullness of time, God has inaugurated the age-to-come, or new creation, promised by the prophets.

The Current Overlap of the Ages

- The inaugurated new age currently overlaps with the present age.

Apocalyptic Intervention, Part II

- In the not-too-distant future, God will act once again, beginning with the return or appearing of Jesus, to end the present age and bring the age-to-come into its glorious fullness.

We may also illustrate this framework as follows:

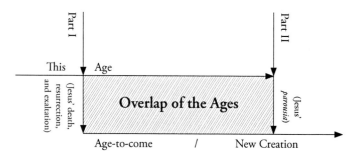

God's Apocalyptic Intervention in Christ

As suggested above, this apocalyptic schema fits into an even broader story that Paul shared with other Jews of his time, a story that begins with creation and ends in re-creation, a story that includes both covenant and new covenant.

"What time is it?" For Paul the time was full, the time was ripe for God to do something new in fulfillment of old promises. That is why Paul is constantly referring to the ancient Scriptures of Israel to understand the new age of Christ and the Spirit. This "something new" will occur in two acts. (We will discuss the content of the two acts in subsequent chapters.) Now, Paul says, we live in the intervening time between the first act and the second act of that dramatic story of divine intervention; we live during the overlap of the ages.

Bifocal Existence in Christ During the Overlap of the Ages

If, as we said in chapter 3, Paul's letters were intended to shape lives and communities, then the focus of his theological reflection, and thus of his letters, will be quite practical. That is, he will be asking and answering the question, "What does it mean to live during the overlap of the ages?" The letter to Titus, like 1 Timothy quoted at the end of chapter 4, captures the dynamic of this question quite well, using forms of the Greek word *epiphaneia* (from which we get "epiphany") to refer to both the first and the second comings—and implying that it is not Caesar's epiphany that saves:

> [11]For the grace of God has appeared [Greek *epephanē*], bringing salvation to all, [12]training us to renounce impiety and worldly passions, and in the present age to live lives that are self-controlled,

> upright, and godly, [13]while we wait for the blessed
> hope and the manifestation [Greek *epiphaneian*] of
> the glory of our great God and Savior, Jesus Christ.
> (Titus 2:11–13)

We will explore the question of living in the overlap of
the ages in more depth in several later chapters, but for now
it is important to note two main points. First, for Paul the
new life is life "in Christ," or "in the Messiah." This phrase,
used dozens of times in Paul's letters, points to a central and
complex dimension of Paul's experience and theology. It suggests not primarily an individual, mystical experience but
the corporate experience of a community shaped by a living,
powerful, personal presence—the resurrected and exalted crucified Messiah. Furthermore, the language can be reversed, as
Paul also experiences the presence of Christ within—Christ in
me/you/us (e.g., Gal 2:20; Rom 8:10; Col 1:27). This is both
a *personal*, though not private, and a *corporate* experience. It is
also described in terms of the indwelling presence of the Spirit
(e.g., Rom 8:9, 11).[2] For Paul, the Spirit is the down-payment
on and guarantee of the fullness of the life to come (2 Cor
1:22; 5:5; Eph 1:13–14), when the final act in God's salvation
drama takes place.

Second, life in Christ during this overlap of the ages is to
be characterized, not surprisingly, by constant careful consideration of both the first act and the second. That is, those in
Christ look both *back* to the past events of incarnation, cross,
and resurrection, on the one hand, and *ahead* to the future
events of return, resurrection, and renewal, on the other. We

2. To further complicate things, Paul can also speak about life in the
Spirit.

might characterize this kind of existence as bifocal—focused on two things, in two directions, so that the present becomes shaped by both the past and the future.[3] To be in Christ, both personally and corporately, is to have one's life, one's story, shaped by the two-part drama of God's apocalyptic intervention. It is to be caught in the middle—a challenging but exciting time to be alive. It is the time in which Christians today find ourselves, too, solidifying our intimate connection with Paul's churches and letters.

About this bifocal existence we will have much more to say. For now, however, we turn our attention to the first part of the drama, beginning with the God whose apocalyptic intervention is the subject of Paul's gospel.

Summary

In this brief chapter we have considered the first of the eight essential Pauline themes, which is itself the overarching framework within which the others are located. The story of God's dream for Israel and for all humanity has come to its climax and is working toward its consummation. That, for Paul, and for us, is indeed good news. This age is passing away, and the new age has begun. To live during the overlap of the ages is to live in a time of great fulfillment and yet also great anticipation. God has acted decisively in Christ and is still on the move by means of the Spirit. It is our privilege and responsibility to be caught up in that divine drama.

3. By "bifocal" I mean having two foci in opposite directions (that is, bi-directional), unlike bifocal glasses that permit one to focus on different objects in the same direction. For one example of how this bifocal vision works, see Paul's treatment of problems surrounding the Lord's supper, in 1 Cor 11:17–34.

Reflection

1. How does Paul's understanding of the word "apocalyptic" differ from common usage of such language, and how is Paul's understanding significant?

2. What do you think should be some of the characteristics of a life, whether that of an individual or a community, lived during the "overlap of the ages" and characterized as a "bifocal" existence oriented toward both God's past and God's future intervention in Christ?

6

"The Gospel of God"

Covenant Faithfulness and Surprising Grace

About a century after Paul, there lived a leader of the early church in Rome named Marcion. Marcion believed that the (allegedly) judgmental and violent "God of the Old Testament" was a different being from the gracious and forgiving "God and Father of our Lord Jesus Christ." Marcion therefore excised the Jewish writers from the developing list of authoritative Christian writings (the New Testament "canon"), leaving Luke and a heavily edited Paul. Marcion tried—unsuccessfully, since it was an impossible task—to remove all the Jewish elements from Paul and to present to the church an un-Jewish God, Paul, and New Testament. He failed at all three, because the majority of the early church's leaders recognized the bankruptcy of his project. Christianity is rooted in Judaism.

It was once famously said of Marcion that he was the only Gentile Christian who ever understood Paul, and he misunderstood him.[1] Although Paul is indeed sometimes difficult to understand, Marcion *definitely* failed to understand Paul; in fact, he betrayed the apostle. From birth to death, Paul believed himself to be serving the one true God of Israel, and of all people, attested in the Jewish Scriptures and revealed

1. German church historian Adolf Harnack, in his 1885 *History of Dogma*, 1:89.

most fully in Jesus the Messiah. Paul's gospel was "the gospel of God" (Rom 1:1, 15:16; 1 Thess 2:2, 8, 9). What does that mean?

The Living God and the Scriptural Witness

In the ancient world Jews distinguished themselves from the majority of their non-Jewish contemporaries in several respects, among which was their belief in and worship of only one God. This one true God was "the living God" (over against nonliving pagan idols), an epithet to which Paul refers several times.[2] This God's name, according to the Scriptures, was YHWH (Yahweh), normally rendered as "the Lord"—*ho kyrios*—in the Greek Bible that Paul and his churches generally used. As we will see in chapter 8, this linguistic phenomenon helped Paul make the connection between Jesus as "Lord" and the God of Israel.

With other Jews, Paul believed that God had spoken the world into existence; called Abraham to be the father of a people, Israel, that would be a blessing to all nations; gave the Law to, and made covenants with, that people; expected the covenant people to obey the precepts of the Law, especially to live in loyalty toward God and in love toward neighbor and stranger, particularly the poor; promised a Messiah to save the people from their sins and oppressors; and spoke through prophets about a future day when God would establish a new, permanent covenant, when sin and injustice would cease, and when even the Gentiles would acknowledge the one true God in a new creation.

2. Rom 9:26, citing Hos 1:10; 2 Cor 3:3; 6:16; 1 Thess 1:9; cf. 1 Tim 3:15; 4:10.

How, then, are we to understand the person we call "God," the divine character, so to speak? Many people, following in the footsteps of Marcion, think that the "Jewish God" or the "God of the Old Testament" is an angry, punitive deity unlike the "Christian God" or the "loving God of the New Testament." This is an inaccurate and dangerous caricature. For Jews in general and for Paul in particular—both before and after his Damascus-Road experience—there are a number of "character traits" that are associated with God:

- God is eternal, God is one, and God is the creator of all;

- God is holy—different in being, character, and action from humans—and God's ways are not our ways;

- God is relational, wanting to be in covenant, or two-way relationship, with people, manifested especially in a chosen people called Israel;

- God is faithful, a maker and keeper of covenant promises;

- God is righteous and just, meaning not only completely fair but especially protective of the weak and oppressed, and committed to restoring the world to wholeness (*shalom*);

- God is gracious, kind, and loving;

- God is demanding, expecting humans to share in the divine holiness, faithfulness, justice, and love;

- God is merciful and forgiving;

- God is a savior, rescuing people from their own follies as well as from oppressors;

- God wishes to establish a people (Israel) and a world where the love of God and neighbor is the order of the day; and

- God is worthy of all honor, praise, and obedience.

This set of beliefs about God's acts and God's "person," or character, derive of course from Israel's Scriptures—especially from Genesis, Deuteronomy, the Psalms, and Isaiah. Various parts of those Scriptures highlight different attributes, but a synthesis of the various parts yields something like the list we have just considered.[3]

Paul was an avid reader and creative interpreter of the Scriptures. Throughout his letters, we find direct citations of the Scriptures, sometimes altered just a bit to make a new point, as well as echoes and less intentional allusions.[4] What do we learn from observing Paul's use of Scripture?

Paul is convinced that in the twin gifts of the Messiah and the Spirit, the story of God's dealings with Israel and the world has come to its climax; the promises and "dreams," so to speak, of Israel's God have been fulfilled. This means that the Scriptures must be re-interpreted in light of this climactic event, and that this climactic event must be interpreted in light of the Scriptures.[5]

3. The caricature of the Old Testament God that many people have is created when certain narratives are lifted from the larger framework of God's character.

4. The foundational study of Paul's use of Scripture is Hays, *Echoes of Scripture*.

5. The use of the word "climax" in this context is due in part to N. T.

As a Jew, both before and after Damascus, Paul saw Israel's Scriptures in general and the Law (the Torah) in particular as God's holy and good gift (Romans 7), including its covenantal demands (the Law's moral and ritual requirements). But after Damascus, Paul also recognized a "dark side" to the Law. Reflecting on his own experience, he found that those who tried to rely on the Law for their justification before God regularly failed to keep it, despite their enthusiasm and pride (Romans 2). Moreover, he found their experience to be a misguided, ineffective, and exclusionary zeal. He concluded that the Law, co-opted by Sin (understood as a power or slave master), could not deliver the life it was intended by God to provide; it could not liberate people from Sin as a power or empower people to fulfill its own demands (Romans 7). And those who persist in following the Law for justification fail to see that it ultimately points to Christ, the Spirit, and the "law" of Christ, the law of faith expressing itself in love (Gal 5:6; 6:2)—in other words, it points to the gospel Paul had experienced and was now proclaiming.

When Jews believed the good news Paul preached, they were believing in the fulfillment of the promises outlined above (Rom 1:2; 15:8; 2 Cor 1:20) and experiencing—truly, though not yet completely—the reality of the prophetically predicted new covenant (1 Cor 11:25; 2 Cor 3:6) and new creation (Gal 6:15; 2 Cor 5:17). When Gentiles believed the gospel, they were turning from pagan idols to the true God (1 Thess 1:9–10) and being graciously incorporated into the people of this God going back to Abraham (Rom 9:19–26; 11:11–24). In effect, they became "spiritual" Jews who, like

---

Wright, beginning with his book *The Climax of the Covenant.*

Jews who believed the gospel, had the foreskin of their *hearts* circumcised in fulfillment of the prophet Jeremiah's vision (Rom 2:28–29; cf. Jer 31:31–34). And that experience of heart surgery, so to speak, made the fulfillment of "the just requirement of the law" possible for Jews and Gentiles alike (Rom 8:4; cf. Ezek 11:19–20; 36:26–27).[6]

Continuity and Creativity

Of the many ways in which Paul appeals to the Scriptures, the most important for our consideration in this chapter is how he identifies—in opposition to Marcion—"the God and Father of our Lord Jesus Christ" (Rom 15:6 and elsewhere) with the God of Israel. It is the God of Israel who has sent the Son and the Spirit in the fullness of time (Gal 4:4–6) to make us members of the covenant people and children of God; it is the God of Israel who has thereby invaded the cosmos to inaugurate the new covenant, new age, and new creation; it is the God of Israel who has demonstrated covenant faithfulness to his own people and remarkable mercy and grace to those who are not his people—the Gentiles. This true story of the true God constitutes the good news of God, a gospel that has to be couched in the language of Scripture, and a gospel that simultaneously sheds new light on the very Scripture it utilizes.

So, for instance, in Romans—which is filled with scriptural quotations—we learn early on (Rom 1:17) that the principle of the just, or righteous, living by faith is not merely

6. Unlike part of the book of Ezekiel, which defines holiness in terms of circumcision of the flesh as well as the heart (Ezek 44:5–9), Paul believes God requires only circumcision of the heart.

sage, pious counsel from a "minor" prophet (Hab 2:4), but rather the key to unlocking how the God of Paul's gospel expects humans to live as the people of God in the world. However, we must not fill words like "just/righteous," "faith," and "live" with our own definitions, or even the definitions of Habakkuk, because Paul's gospel reinterprets those terms, loading them with a surplus of meaning that they did not have for Habbakuk and might not have for us—unless we rightly understand the rest of Romans.

Similarly, when in 1 Cor 1:31 Paul cites Jeremiah (Jer 9:24) about boasting in the Lord, he takes a very important prophetic precept and turns it into a subversive text summarizing, from a new perspective, the call of the gospel. The text from Jeremiah is intended by Paul to deconstruct the Corinthians' communal misbehavior and re-orient them toward the *crucified* Lord Jesus as the new way of "boasting" in the God of Israel—a way unknown to Jeremiah, but spelled out in 1 Cor 1:18–25. In Paul's preaching and letter-writing, Scriptural words and realities like "faith" and even "God" ("the Lord") are constantly being subjected to the reconstructing work of the gospel.

That point leads us to an important caveat in the consideration of Paul's gospel as the gospel of God: God is the same and yet different. The experience of the Messiah and the Spirit have affected what Paul means when he utters the word "God"; there is both continuity and discontinuity with his past experience and understanding. We consider this subject here, but we will also return to it in later chapters.[7]

---

7. Especially to focus on Paul's inclusion of Jesus in the divine identity (chapter 8).

God the Father, the Son, and the Spirit

In a famous passage in Galatians (4:4–6), Paul claims that God first sent his Son into the world to make us children of God, and then sent the Spirit of the Son into our hearts to make that new relationship a lived experience of calling God "Abba"—the same Aramaic word for "Father" that Jesus would have used. The text obviously suggests an intimate interconnection among three "actors" in addition to the human recipients of this grace: God the Father, the Son, and the Spirit of the Son—elsewhere also called the Spirit of God.[8]

Later Christian thinkers would develop a complex theology of this interrelationship in the doctrine of the Trinity, the basic notion being the existence of one God in three "persons." It is often argued that to attribute anything resembling a Trinitarian conception of God to Paul is to read him anachronistically, projecting later theology onto the New Testament documents. This argument is perhaps understandable for a variety of reasons, but it is seriously misguided. To be sure, Paul does not use the philosophical and theological language of the later church fathers who developed the doctrine of the Trinity for their times. However, had the later church not articulated the doctrine of the Trinity, it would have failed to grapple fully and satisfactorily with the witness of Paul. As N. T. Wright has said with respect to Paul's understanding of God, "one might conclude that if the doctrine of the Trinity had not come into existence it would be necessary to invent it."[9]

8. "Spirit of God" occurs eight times, including Rom 8:9, where it appears with "Spirit of Christ."

9. Wright, *Paul: In Fresh Perspective*, 98.

We find in Paul a stream of texts in which he either articulates a conception and an experience of God as three-in-one or he attributes to the Son and/or the Spirit traits and activities that the Jewish Scriptures associate with God. In other words, Paul's experience of the Son and the Spirit has caused him to read the Scriptures afresh and to articulate anew precisely who God is and how God is known. Since we will deal with some of the texts discussing the Son and the Spirit individually in later chapters, here we will briefly mention some aspects of God as "three-in-one" in Paul's letters.[10]

In Rom 5:1–11, Paul says that justification is an experience of reconciliation, peace, and love made possible by God, Christ, and the Spirit. Like Gal 4:4–6, this passage suggests a two-stage manifestation of God's activity on our behalf, described in this passage as the revelation of God's reconciling and saving love that gives hope to its recipients. That love of God is manifested objectively in the death of Christ (5:8) and known experientially in the gift of the Holy Spirit (5:5). God's gracious love is known, in other words, in the interrelated activity of the Father, the Son, and the Spirit. In a similar vein but with different language, Paul describes the conversion of the Thessalonians as their turning to "the living and true God" in response to what he calls "the word of the Lord [Jesus]" in the power and inspiration of the Spirit (1 Thess 1:2–10).

That divine, three-in-one activity is not only in the past. Paul claims that the three-in-one God continues to work

10. See further Gorman, *Cruciformity*, 63–74, and the additional sources cited there. The claim being made here is that Paul *experienced* God as three-in-one (what theologians call the "economic Trinity") and that failure to acknowledge this causes multiple misunderstandings of Paul. See slso Fee, *Empowering Presence*, 841–45; Dunn, *Theology*, 264.

in the assembly of believers, where the Spirit enables those who are in Christ to discern and do the will of God (1 Thess 5:12–22). Similarly, in 1 Corinthians 12 Paul uses parallel phrases to indicate the distinct but interrelated action of the three-in-one God in the experience of spiritual gifts: the Spirit gives, the Lord [Jesus] is served, and God [the Father] is at work (1 Cor 12: 4–6).

Elsewhere in Paul's letters we find further evidence that he sees the gospel as enabling an experience of God as three-in-one. Romans 8 is perhaps the most comprehensive statement of that reality, as Paul, using vivid metaphors and images, richly portrays life in Christ as life in the Spirit and life as God's adopted children. The ultimate goal of that life is Spirit-empowered conformity to the Son and thus a share in the inheritance of "glory" that is Christ's as the "firstborn" in God's family—the one "unadopted" child (Rom 8:14–17, 29–30). This transforming activity of God, the Spirit, and the Lord is noted explicitly in several additional Pauline texts (e.g., 2 Cor 3:12–18; Phil 2:1–13) and is assumed throughout the letters.

Paul's God is, in other words, three-in-one, the reconfigured God of Israel and its Scriptures. This is the "God" in "the gospel of God." This is the God Paul experiences and announces in his gospel: the God of faithfulness and mercy, the God of love and grace.

God Faithful and Gracious

Of all the divine character traits Paul celebrates, among the most prominent—and paradoxical—are God's faithfulness and God's grace. As noted above, Paul learned of these traits from Israel's Scriptures, and he saw them displayed afresh in the actions of the three-in-one God known now in Jesus the Messiah (e.g., Rom 3:21–26; 5:6–8).

For Paul, both God's faithfulness and God's grace are rooted in God's promises (Rom 4:11–17). God's plan and promise was to bless both the chosen people, Israel, and all nations through Abraham and his descendants. But human folly and sin interfered with that plan. God's response, throughout Israel's history and culminating in the gift of the Messiah, was to act with covenant faithfulness to the promises made and with surprising mercy, or grace (unmerited favor), toward human sin. God's action, in and through the gospel, is to faithfully show mercy by making peace with and for a rebellious humanity. This is, arguably, the primary theological theme of Paul's most theological letter, Romans. For Paul (see Romans 9–11), it is equally a surprising act of faithfulness and grace that God neither gives up on hard-hearted Israel nor excludes those who were not originally "my people" (Rom 9:25–26, referring to Gentiles, in a reinterpretation of Hosea).

"Grace and peace" therefore become the hallmark of Paul's experience of God, and the experience he wishes others to have. He begins and ends all of his letters with benedictions containing one or both of these words, wrapping whatever he says in reminders of the fundamental nature of both God and the gospel.[11] The letters also summarize everything God has done in Christ as "the grace of God" (2 Cor 6:1; Col 1:6) and the "appearing" of the grace of God (Tit 2:11), while also

11. Rom 1:7; 15:13, 33; 16:20; 1 Cor 1:3–4; 16:23; 2 Cor 1:2, 12; 13:13; Gal 1:3–6, 6:16–18; Eph 1:2–7, 6:23–24; Phil 1:2; 4:7–9, 23; Col 1:6; 4:18; 1 Thess 1:1; 5:28; 2 Thess 1:2; 3:18; 1 Tim 1:2; 6:21; 2 Tim 1:2; 4:22; Tit 1:4; 3:15; Phlm 3, 25.

calling God "the God of peace" (Rom 15:33; 16:20; Phil 4:9;
1 Thess 5:23) who provides the "peace of God" (Phil 4:7).
This is clearly something other than the Pax Romana—or the
Pax Americana. Yet this peace is not merely private ("how to
have peace with God"), for it is the *shalom* of God promised
by the prophets, a peace with real-world consequences (Mic
5:4–5; Isa 2:2–4, 9:2–7). The letters also characterize Christ
as our peace (Eph 2:14), and the "peace of Christ" as central
to Christian experience (Col 3:15).[12]

God's peace and grace, then, come to fullest expression
for Paul in Christ (Rom 5:15; 1 Cor 1:4). This is so crucial
for Paul that he can even speak of God's grace as the grace of
our Lord Jesus Christ.[13] God's grace is a reconciling, peacemaking, and transforming power. The focal point of this
grace in Christ is, of course, the death of Christ (Gal 2:21),
where God's faithfulness and mercy come into full view (Rom
3:21–26).

Summary

There is little doubt that Paul came to his conclusions about
God through a combination of experience and rereading the
Scriptures in light of that experience. Scriptural talk of realities
like the grace or mercy of God (e.g., Hosea), the Son's being at
God's right hand (e.g., Psalm 110), and the Spirit's remaking
of human hearts (e.g., Jeremiah 31) had become real to Paul
in the appearance of Jesus to him, and in the subsequent expe-

12. The importance of peace in Paul and in the New Testament
more generally has not always been noted. For a corrective, see Swartley,
Covenant of Peace.

13. See Gal 6:18 and other concluding benedictions, plus 2 Cor 8:9
("generous act" in the NRSV).

riences, enabled by the Spirit, of those to whom he preached the gospel of God. These experiences made sense only as the unified activity of the one true God to benevolently, peaceably invade the world in order to redeem it, with faithfulness and grace, in the fullness of time—the time of the Messiah and the Spirit, the onset of the new age. The focal point of that gospel of God was the crucified Messiah, to which we turn in the next chapter, for, as N. T. Wright has said, "the cross of Jesus the Messiah stands at the heart of Paul's vision of the one true God."[14]

Reflection

1. In what ways do we still see the ideas of Marcion present today?

2. Why is it important for Paul and for us that the God of Israel's Scriptures is (1) the God and Father of our Lord Jesus Christ and (2) "three-in-one," reconfigured around Christ and the Spirit?

3. Paul is well known for his emphasis on grace, but perhaps less so for his emphasis on peace, not only with God but also with others. Why are grace and peace so central to the Christian gospel?

14. N. T. Wright, *Paul: In Fresh Perspective*, 96.

7

"Even Death on a Cross"

The Meaning(s) of Christ's Death

⌘ Most people readily identify the cross as the distinctive symbol of the Christian faith. Christians go a step further, acknowledging the cross as the source of their own salvation, confessing that "Christ died for me." The reality and the doctrine of the cross—what theologians call the "atonement" (at-one-ment)—is at the center of Christian existence and therefore of Christian singing. Old hymns speak of "cherishing" and "clinging to" the cross. Contemporary music says much the same thing, only in a different idiom. Christians cherish the cross because that is where Christ died for them and their sins.

For most Christians, then, the cross they sing about has a very important and appropriate focus, but a fairly narrow one. For Paul, on the other hand, the cross—or more specifically the Crucified and his story—is a comprehensive reality, the breadth and depth of which can never be exhausted. Its significance is so far-reaching that Paul can refer to his gospel as the "word of the cross" (1 Cor 1:18; NRSV: "message of the cross"), and he can claim to know and preach nothing but "Christ crucified" (1 Cor 2:2). The cross is not only the *source* of life with and in God/Christ/the Spirit, but also the *shape* of that life. Moreover—and this will be surprising to some—for

Paul the cross is not just an act of Jesus Christ; it is a revelation of *God*. In fact, it is the definitive divine self-revelation.

We find in Paul, therefore, a wide variety of interpretations, images, and insights about the death of Jesus the Messiah and its significance for understanding God, being reconciled to God through the Messiah, and living "in" the Messiah by the power of the Spirit. Paul draws on one interpretation here and another there, apparently choosing the one(s) most appropriate for the larger pastoral point he is trying to make. We can safely assume that he finds them all complementary, rather than mutually exclusive, even when he focuses on one. Thus it is helpful to know something of the variety of Paul's interpretations of the cross as we read specific texts that reflect one or more of them.

Whenever we read *any* of these interpretations of Christ's death on the cross,[1] we must keep in mind that the cross was not a template for pretty jewelry in the Roman world. Rather, as we have already noted, the cross was a sign of Roman power. Crucifixion was a way of punishing non-citizens who threatened the fabric of Rome by exposing them in public as the weight of Roman "justice" crushed their weakened bodies. No deity and no Jewish messiah worthy of his salt would be a *crucified* messiah or a *crucified* god.

Except one.

---

1. Paul does not always refer explicitly to the cross/crucifixion of Christ when he discusses his death—but it is implied even when it is not specified.

The Cross and God

It would seem normal to start a discussion of "Christ crucified" with Christ—but we are starting with God. That is because for Paul the unseen—or, better, the unveiled—actor in Christ's death on the cross is God—the same God of Israel we considered in the previous chapter. How is this so?

Paul claims that "in Christ God was reconciling the world to himself" (2 Cor 5:19). Although this could refer more broadly to Christ's entire life as God's means of reconciliation, the context suggests that Paul is focusing on Christ's death as God's initiative to win back the world. In another text on Christ's death as God's act of reconciliation (Rom 5:1–11), Paul stresses that *Christ's* death was *God's* act of love (Rom 5:8)—an odd claim indeed unless there is something quite intimate about the relationship between God and Christ (cf. Col 1:19–22). It is also quite strange in another way—the cross is an emblem of suffering and shame, of imperial violence and deterrence—hardly a sign of love. "It took genius to see that the symbol which had spoken of Caesar's naked might now spoke of God's naked love," claims N. T. Wright.[2] Paul tells us that God "did not withhold his own Son, but gave him up for all of us" (Rom 8:32), and that God "put [Christ Jesus] forward as a sacrifice of atonement by his blood" (Rom 3:25; cf. Rom 8:3; 2 Cor 5:21). God's gift of his own Son demonstrates for Paul that God is both faithful to the covenant and righteous, finding a way to deal with the matter of human rebellion and sin (Rom 3:21–26), even when we were God's *enemies* (Rom 5:6–10). That is amazing grace, amazing love.

2. Wright, *Paul: In Fresh Perspective*, 73.

(None of this means, of course, that Christ was uninvolved, a mere passive agent, an object of divine manipulation; we will say more about that momentarily.)

In Paul's view, then, the cross actually tells us something about God's character, God's attributes as God. The death of Jesus is not an anomaly—a onetime, quirky expression of divine love. Nor is it only the Father's gift of the Son to us—a "three-party" transaction.[3] Rather, in a profound sense, the cross is God's own act of self-giving: "God was in Christ."

The cross reveals the way God *is* by revealing the way God works in the world: through foolishness and weakness, at least as they are normally measured, rather than through wisdom and might, at least as they are normally measured. Christ, Paul says, is "the power of God and the wisdom of God" (1 Cor 1:24), and in context, this can only mean that Christ *crucified* is the power and wisdom of God. The crucified Messiah "became for us wisdom from God, and righteousness and sanctification and redemption" (1 Cor 1:30). That is, God's traditional attributes (wisdom, power, justice, holiness, etc.) are revealed on the cross in radically nontraditional ways.

This claim means, then, that the cross is a divine revelation—a theophany. In it we see the face of God—the face of sacrificial love, powerful weakness, and wise folly that redeems the world. It is, for Paul and for us, a mystery and a paradox—but it is the heart of the gospel.[4]

3. Still less is the cross for Paul an act of divine punishment, even divine child abuse, as some have argued.

4. Karl Barth claims that "the proper being of the one true God [is] . . . in Jesus Christ the Crucified. . . . Granted that we do see and understand this, we cannot refuse to accept the humiliation and lowliness

The Cross and Christ

Paul's view of the cross as theophany does not exclude Christ's role. His role is, in fact, part of the paradox and the mystery: how can the cross be both the work of God and the experience of a human being? Of the several interpretations of Christ and the cross in Paul, we will consider two: his cross as sacrifice and as covenant-fulfilling faith and love.

Perhaps the simplest, starkest affirmation about the meaning of Christ's death in the New Testament is the Pauline idiom "Christ died for us/for our sins/for the ungodly/for all/for me," which appears in these and similar variations throughout the letters.[5] In these texts, Christ appears as a sacrifice for sin, building on the many Scriptural texts about various kinds of sacrifices for sin. Paul draws on these various biblical traditions about sacrifice in other ways, too. For example, he calls Christ the sacrificed paschal (Passover) lamb (1 Cor 5:7). He also designates Christ as the God-given means of dealing with sin (Rom 8:3); the "sacrifice of atonement" (NRSV, NIV) or perhaps "expiation" (NAB) for sins (Rom 3:25);[6] and the sinless one whom God "made. . . to be sin" for our sake (2 Cor 5:21). And Paul alludes both to the near-sacrifice of Isaac by

---

and supremely the obedience of Christ as the dominating moment in our conception of God. Therefore we must determine to seek and find the key to the whole . . . concept of the 'divine nature' at the point where it appears to be quite impossible . . . [i.e., in] the fact that Jesus Christ was obedient unto death, even the death of the cross" (*Church Dogmatics* IV/1, 199). Paul, I am arguing, would agree.

5. Rom 5:6, 8; 1 Cor 15:3; 2 Cor 5:14–15; Gal 1:4; 2:20; etc.

6. The translation of this verse is notoriously difficult; a less likely rendering is "propitiation," meaning that which turns away God's wrath.

Abraham (Rom 8:32) and to the sin-bearing death of Isaiah's suffering servant (Phil 2:7–8) in describing Christ's death.

This sacrificial language does not mean, however, that Christ is an unwilling participant, a mere variable in the equation of divine justice. Rather, Paul presents Christ's death as the ultimate covenantal expression of his obedience and faithfulness to God, on the one hand, and his self-giving love for us, on the other.

In the famous poetic text found in Philippians, Paul says that Christ Jesus "became obedient to the point of death—even death on a cross" (Phil 2:8); the obedience is clearly to God. This finale was the conclusion of a life-story of self-emptying, self-giving obedience and, Paul implies from the context (Phil 2:1–4), self-emptying, self-giving love:

> . . . *though* he was in the form of God,
> [he] *did not* regard equality with God
>> as something to be exploited [for his own advantage],
> *but* emptied himself,
>> taking the form of a slave,
>> being born in human likeness.
>> And being found in human form,
> he humbled himself
> and became obedient to the point of death—
>> even death on a cross. (Phil 2:6–8)

This text is famous for the phrase "emptied himself," referring to Christ's utter abandonment of self in service to God and others that theologians call "kenosis," from the noun form of the Greek verb "to empty." The italicized connecting words in this text from Philippians (*though. . . did not. . . but*) represent a common pattern in Paul's letters that indicates the essence of self-emptying, "kenotic," or "cruciform" (cross-shaped) love: although [x] not [y] but [z], meaning *although* [x] one possesses a certain status, one *does not* [y] exploit it for selfish gain *but* [z] acts for the good of others.

Similarly, in Galatians, Paul describes the Lord Jesus Christ as the one who "gave himself for our sins to set us free from the present evil age, according to the will of our God and Father" (Gal 1:4), and as the one who expressed his faithfulness to God when he "loved me by giving himself for me" (Gal 2:20; my translation). Both texts suggest an act of loyalty to God as well as love for us. Christ's death is characterized as his faithfulness to God in other places, too (Rom 3:22; Gal 3:22; Phil 3:9), and, similarly, as his obedience/act of righteousness (Rom 5:18–19).[7] And it is celebrated as an act of love from which we benefit (2 Cor 5:14–15).

In other words, for Paul the cross is the quintessential, unified act of loyalty to God and love for others—what Paul, like Jesus, understands to be the essence of the Jewish Law, the covenant obligations for God's people to love God and neighbor.[8] This perspective will form the foundation of Paul's understanding of the appropriate human response to the gos-

7. As noted in chapter 4, this interpretation of Christ's death as his act of faithfulness to God depends on reading a Greek phrase, normally translated "faith in" Christ/the Son of God, as "the faith of" Christ/the Son of God. This alternate translation appears in some footnotes (e.g., in the NRSV) and is now incorporated in the text of the NET (New English Translation) Bible, an online version (www.bible.org/netbible) available also in print form. It has become the preferred interpretation of many Pauline scholars.

8. Cf. Mark 12:28–34.

pel—a unified response of faith and love—as God's way of forming a (new) covenant community.

It must be stressed that Christ's obedience to God is, paradoxically, freely chosen: he emptied and humbled *himself;* this freedom is part of the paradox of covenant loyalty. Such loyalty, rooted in the Scriptural vision of Israel's relationship to YHWH made possible by the Exodus, is a *bonded* freedom. It is also why Paul can say that those who love are truly free inasmuch as they are freely bound to others (Gal 5:1, 13–26).

To summarize: as Christ's own act, the cross is the needed and effective sacrifice for sin, and it is the manifestation of Christ's covenant faithfulness (loyalty, obedience) toward God and covenant love toward us. The death of Jesus is thus the quintessential act of covenant fulfillment, completing the "vertical" (faith toward God) and "horizontal" (love toward neighbor) demands of the covenant. We identify with and participate in this act through co-crucifixion with Christ in faith and baptism, and are thereby justified (Gal 2:15–21). (We will say more about this below and in chapter 9 on justification.)

The Cross and the Human Condition

That the cross is ultimately an act of God and of Christ "for us" means that the cross tells us also something about us, about what we often refer to as the "human condition." On this subject Paul speaks with both a traditional and a creative Jewish voice.

As noted above and in concert with other Jews of his era, including Jesus, Paul believes that God expects people to live in covenant relation with God and with others: to love God and neighbor. Also with other Jews, he especially finds Gentiles, or pagans, lacking in these two departments, characterizing their life in terms of *idolatry* instead of worship of God and in terms of *immorality* and *injustice* instead of neighbor-love (Rom 1:18–32; 1 Cor 5:9–12; 6:9–11). Like Israel's prophets (e.g., Jeremiah 7, Hosea), Paul applies this critique also to Israel, concluding that these two fundamental sins and their various manifestations are not peculiar to non-Jews but are the lot of the entire human family, even Jews (Rom 2:1—3:20). Humans constantly break covenant: they worship false gods and disobey the true God; engage in sex in unnatural ways and for selfish ends; lie, cheat, and steal; practice all kinds of violence; and condone others who do the same![9] Their "vertical" and "horizontal" relationships are all disordered.

Paul posits a startling and creative explanation for this moral chaos, this carnival of sins in the world. Behind and within all the sins (plural) is a power that Paul calls Sin (singular; Rom 3:9), a force within the human person and the human family that fundamentally enslaves us (Rom 6:6–7), such that we habitually cannot do what is right, even if and when we want to (Rom 7:7–24). Our situation is like that of the addict, and Sin is our drug of choice—or, better said, our Master. That we are addicted does not excuse our behavior, but it does suggest in no uncertain terms that we cannot cure ourselves. We are, so to speak, *covenantally dysfunctional*, neither loyal to God nor loving to neighbor.

9. For a sustained treatment of Paul's view, see Romans 1:18—3:20 as a whole, and/or read the daily news for supporting evidence.

The consequences of this condition are very serious. Paul describes the human condition as one of death (Rom 6:13; cf. Col 2:13; Eph 2:1–5), vividly referring to the consequences of sin as the "wages" it pays, namely, death (Rom 6:21–23). Paul attributes this situation both to the disobedience of the first human (Adam) and to our perpetual confirmation of that rebellion toward God (Rom 5:12). By "death," then, Paul means both a present spiritual state of deadness toward God and the future reality of physical death, both the result of sin. The great and powerful enemies of the human race are Sin and Death, which are real characters in the human drama as Paul depicts it (Rom 7:7–13; 1 Cor 15:26, 51–57).

Thus we live in an age dominated by Sin and by sins, a spell with grave consequences—death and Death—that can be broken only by a divine action that addresses both problems: Sin and sins, the one and the many.[10] We need both forgiveness and liberation. For Paul, Christ's death accomplishes both: it is God's way of both forgiving our sins (plural) and liberating us from the power of Sin (singular) by defeating its death-dealing power (Rom 3:21–26; 8:1–4). The "mechanics" of this salvation/solution are not Paul's main concern, though he describes Christ's death from a variety of angles, as we have seen; he is interested above all in the effects.

10. Although the cross and resurrection cannot really be separated any more than sin and death can be separated, the cross deals more directly with sin and the resurrection more directly with death. As we will see in the next chapter, Christ's resurrection permits both our resurrection to new life now and our future resurrection/eternal life.

The results, or benefits, of Christ's death for us are manifold in Paul's thinking. We can name a few of the most important:[11]

- justification, or the restoration of right covenant relations on our part toward God and others (e.g., Rom 3:24–31; 5:1–11; 8:30; 10:10; 1 Cor 6:11; Gal 2:15–21; 3:6–11);

- reconciliation, or the cessation of enmity and the restoration of friendship with God and others (Rom 5:1–11; 2 Cor 5:18–21; Eph 2:11–22);

- redemption, or release from bondage to Sin (singular) and return to our proper owner (Rom 3:24; 1 Cor 6:19–20);

- forgiveness of sins (plural; Rom 3:25; 4:7; 1 Cor 15:3; Gal; 1:4; Col 1:14);

- deliverance from oppressive cosmic powers, which have been defeated by the cross (Col 2:13–15);

- deliverance from the coming wrath of God on the day of the Lord (the day of judgment and salvation; Rom 5:9–11; 1 Thess 1:10);

- empowerment to fulfill the covenant's obligations (Rom 8:3–4).

One way that Paul expresses these results or benefits is in the metaphorical language of interchange: God made the sinless Christ become sin, so that we might become God's righteousness in him (2 Cor 5:21); Christ became poor so that we

11. For a classic discussion, see Fitzmyer, *Paul and his Theology*, 55–71.

might become rich (2 Cor 8:9). Early Christian theologians after Paul, beginning with Irenaeus in the late second century, would summarize this Pauline theme in the following way: "He became what we were so that we might become what he is." We only benefit from Christ's death by participating in it, as we will explore further in later chapters.

Summary

For Paul the cross is an act of both God's love and Christ's love; it is God's sacrificial gift and Christ's sacrificial obedience; it is the revelation of God's faithfulness and character as well as the quintessential expression of Christ's covenant faithfulness. Through it, God reconciles, justifies, redeems, forgives, transforms, and much more.

The cross is an invitation to see God and ourselves in a new light, the light of paradox and mystery, the light of loyalty and love, the light of life through death. The inadequacy of much Christian hymnody in referring to the all-encompassing cross too narrowly—to which we made reference at the beginning of this chapter—is perhaps addressed by the appropriateness of at least one hymn text: the last stanza of "When I Survey the Wondrous Cross":

> Were the whole realm of nature mine,
> That were a present far too small;
> Love so amazing, so divine,
> Demands my soul, my life, my all.

But of course, without the resurrection, the cross would be meaningless. It would simply be the foolish, shameful death of a messianic pretender and possible threat to the Roman status quo—not the death of the Son of God and Lord of glory (1 Cor 2:8). So we turn now to the resurrection.

Reflection

1. What difference does it make to begin a conversation about the cross with God?

2. How could seeing the cross as the definitive theophany impact our understanding of God, Christ, ourselves, the church, the world, and the cross itself?

3. In what ways is faithfulness a part of the comprehensive reality of the cross?

4. Why and how does the cross get misinterpreted by both Christians and non-Christians?

8

"God Raised" and
"Highly Exalted Him"

Jesus is Son of God and Lord

✣ In the previous chapter we saw that the cross of Christ has multiple meanings. We must now emphatically say that the cross of Christ is in fact *meaningless* for Paul, and for us, apart from the resurrection. For Paul, God's resurrection of Christ is the validation, vindication, and completion of the cross. It makes the cross a victory rather than a defeat. It means that Jesus is exalted to the "right hand" of God and is Messiah, Son of God, Savior, and Lord. The resurrection is the source of power and new life in the present, as well as hope for the future.

In chapter 2 we briefly outlined how Paul came to believe in the resurrection of Christ and all that it means. In this chapter, following the pattern of the previous one, we explore more fully the meaning of the resurrection for God, for Christ, and for us. But we begin with a simple question: Why does the resurrection matter so much?

Why the Resurrection Matters

Paul's most direct answer to that question comes to us as part of his fullest treatment of the resurrection of Christ and of

1

believers, which appears in 1 Corinthians 15. Some believers in the Christ-assembly at Corinth, although they had learned from Paul an early Christian creedal narrative that affirmed Christ's resurrection (1 Cor 15:3–5), apparently denied the reality/possibility of resurrection in principle, or at least denied a future general resurrection (1 Cor 15:12). Paul pulls out all the logical, theological, and rhetorical stops to respond to these naysayers (1 Cor 15:12–34).

He starts with the negative consequences of denying resurrection (1 Cor 15:13–19, 30–32): if there is no resurrection, then Christ has not been raised and is therefore obviously still, and permanently, dead; Paul's proclamation and the Corinthians' faith are empty and in vain, and preachers like Paul misrepresent God; forgiveness of sins is an illusion because the cross has no divine vindication and hence no saving significance; dead believers in Christ are gone forever; and living believers who have a resurrection hope are gullible, pitiable folks who ought instead to "eat and drink, for tomorrow we die" (1 Cor 15:32). Moreover, the life of suffering service Paul leads is foolish. These are serious—and perfectly logical—consequences.

But Paul then switches to the positive consequences that flow from Christ's resurrection (1 Cor 15:20–34, 50–58). He focuses on the future consequences and their impact on daily life: Christ's resurrection is the "first fruits" of the future, general resurrection, the guarantee of resurrection for those who have died in Christian hope; death will one day be destroyed; and thus Christian faith, preaching, life, and labor, including suffering, are *not* in vain. Underlying these explicit consequences is the implicit affirmation that the resurrection is the

linchpin in the creed cited at the beginning of 1 Corinthians
15. The resurrection guarantees that the crucified and buried
Jesus really is God's messiah (Christ) and the universal Lord;
that his death really was God's provision for sin; and that the
"church" is really not the enemy of Israel's God but rather the
gracious creation of that God.

God and the Logic of the Resurrection

As we noted in chapter 2, perhaps the main reasons the pre-
Damascus Paul wanted to eliminate the fledgling church were
(1) its preaching of a crucified, and thereby cursed, Messiah
and (2) its embrace of Gentiles in a way that polluted Israel.
That is, he disassociated God from the crucified Messiah and
the church. What turned Paul the persecutor around was the
appearance to him of the resurrected Christ, an encounter he
compared to that of the original apostles (1 Cor 9:1; 15:5–11;
cf. Gal 1:12). What went through Paul's mind—over some
period of time, by means of divine revelation and inspiration—as a result of this experience? How did it change his
view of what God was doing in Israel and the world?

Paul knew that Jesus had been crucified by the Romans.
When Jesus appeared to him, Paul learned that Jesus was obviously no longer dead. Since Jesus was no longer dead, then
he had been raised from the dead, and since only God can
raise the dead, as every Pharisee knew, Jesus must have been
raised from the dead *by God*. That is why Paul almost always
says, not "he rose," but "God raised him" or "he was raised."[1]

1. That is, by God the Father and/or the Father working through the
Spirit. See Rom 4:24; 6:4–9; 7:4; 8:11, 34; 10:9; 1 Cor 6:14; 15:4, 12–20;
2 Cor 4:14; 5:15; Gal 1:1; Eph 1:20; Col 2:12; 1 Thess 1:10; 2 Tim 2:8.
(1 Thess 4:14 is the only exception, and that may reflect a pre-Pauline
acclamation.)

(1) The first major consequence of Paul's realization was a thorough revision of his estimation of the cross and the Crucified. Since God had raised just this one man from the dead, this resurrected one must have some special status in God's plan and should now be seen, first of all, as God's vindicated righteous servant who atones for our sin, like the famous suffering servant:

> [13]See, my [God's] servant shall prosper; he shall be exalted and lifted up, and shall be very high. . . . [4]Surely he has borne our [the people's] infirmities and carried our diseases; yet we accounted him stricken, struck down by God, and afflicted. [5]But he was wounded for our transgressions, crushed for our iniquities; upon him was the punishment that made us whole, and by his bruises we are healed. . . . [12]Therefore I [God] will allot him a portion with the great, and he shall divide the spoil with the strong; because he poured out himself to death, and was numbered with the transgressors; yet he bore the sin of many, and made intercession for the transgressors. (Isa 52:13; 53:4–5, 12)

Paul especially appeals to this text in the poem found in Phil 2:6–11, which is essentially a reinterpretation of Isaiah's suffering-servant poem in light of Jesus. In fact, the absence of the words "raised" and "resurrection" in Phil 2:6–11 but the presence of the phrase "highly exalted" (Phil 2:9) is almost certainly due to the similar language in Isa 52:13 cited above. The resurrection was Jesus' exaltation (see further below).

God's resurrection of Jesus vindicated and validated him, especially marking his death by crucifixion as redemptive and revelatory. Moreover, if Jesus' crucifixion has been vindicated and validated by God, then clearly his cross must not ultimately be a sign of divine curse but a means of divine blessing (Gal 3:13–14).[2] Furthermore, the early church's otherwise absurd claim that the crucified Jesus is God's appointed Messiah and Son actually makes sense. And if the crucified Jesus is the Messiah, then God's way of saving Israel and redeeming the world is not by inflicting violence, but by absorbing it. Moreover, God's activity in the world is characterized by exercising power through powerlessness and bringing life through death.

(2) The second major consequence for Paul involved a reevaluation of the Gentiles and their relation to God and Israel. Since the resurrection of the dead is an *eschatological* event (one associated with the "end times" or "last things"), but God has raised this one man from the dead *now*, then Jesus' resurrection must signal the beginning of the eschatological age and the general resurrection anticipated by Pharisees like Paul. (Paul creatively uses the image of Christ's resurrection as the "first fruits" of a harvest: 1 Cor 15:20–23.) Since the eschatological age has begun, the Jewish people must be experiencing the eschatological promise of new exodus and new covenant made by the prophets, and the Gentiles must be about to come to the knowledge of the true God, as the prophets (and Jewish tradition) also taught.

Since, however, the resurrection of the One has occurred, but the resurrection of the many has not, there must now be an in-between time before the eschatological age comes in

2. There is of course a divine paradox here, as in the theology of "interchange" discussed in the previous chapter. Christ's being made a curse "for us" is, paradoxically, the ultimate blessing.

full—the overlap of the ages we discussed in chapter 5. The primary purpose of this time between the past resurrection of the Messiah and the future general resurrection will be to renew Israel—though Israel will largely resist—and bring the gospel to the Gentiles, creating an "Israel of God" (Gal 6:16) consisting of ethnic Jews and Gentiles who together embrace the Messiah.[3]

The personal consequences for Paul's new understanding of God in Christ, as a result of the resurrection, were of course profound. Since God's way of saving the world is by absorbing violence rather than inflicting it, then those who know and experience that salvation begin a new life of sharing in the crucified Messiah's sufferings rather than inflicting suffering on those who follow him. That is, they are called to a life marked by exercising power through powerlessness and bringing about life through death. Paul discerned that his own life would henceforth be one that, paradoxically, displays the power of the resurrection by being marked with the sign of the cross.[4] This will be the norm for all who have died and risen with Christ, as we will see more fully in subsequent chapters, but especially for apostles. Moreover, since the Gentiles are about to come to the knowledge of the true God before the general resurrection, Paul's role as persecutor of the church must be transformed into a life of bringing the good news of

3. See Romans 9–11 for the dynamic relationship between Jewish rejection and Gentile acceptance of the gospel.

4. For example, Paul will forego his right to financial support and take the cultural risk of shaming himself by doing manual labor to support himself rather than burden the churches; see 1 Corinthians 9; 1 Thessalonians 2.

the crucified and resurrected Messiah, not only to Israel but also, and especially, to the Gentiles.

Paul, then, continued to hold on to his Jewish belief that God is the one who raises the dead (Rom 4:17; 2 Cor 1:9). But his evaluation of the crucified Jesus, of Gentiles, and of his own role in God's story was transfigured by the resurrection of the one he would call God's Son, and our Lord.

Christ and the Resurrection: The Exalted and Present Lord

What, next, does the resurrection say about Christ? Obviously, it means that Christ is alive. This living Christ is, paradoxically, both present in his assemblies and present with God, exalted as Son of God and Lord.

The resurrection of Christ that Paul preached was a real, bodily resurrection—not some modern "resurrection of his spirit" or ongoing "living forever in the hearts of his loved ones." This sort of notion of resurrection from the dead, or the idea, both ancient and modern, of the immortality of a soul-less body, would have never entered the mind of a Pharisee. Moreover, the language of "appearance" that Paul uses as confirmation of Christ's resurrection implies the presence of someone who can be seen and of a seeing that is sometimes experienced as a public event (1 Cor 9:1; 15:5–8). The words Paul often utilizes to describe the resurrection literally mean that God raised Christ "from among the dead ones" (e.g., Rom 4:24; 6:4, 9; 8:11; 10:7). Thus Paul's references to resurrection and appearance are literal, not metaphorical, and the events described are concrete and visible, not mystical and invisible.[5]

Although Christ's resurrection was bodily, it was not a mere resuscitation of his corpse, because resurrection for Paul means also transformation. Christ has been transformed, from having a normal body to having a "spiritual," "glorified" body (1 Cor 15:42–50; Phil 3:21).[6] In Christ's case, this transformed body is apparently no longer limited by time and space, as his appearances demonstrate.[7]

This living, exalted Christ does not, however, simply make "guest appearances," so to speak. In fact, Paul implies that Christ's last resurrection appearance was the one to him (1 Cor 15:8). Now, however, Christ takes up residence in individuals and assemblies, while individuals and communities simultaneously inhabit him. (This mode of residing in and among people is by the agency of the Spirit: Rom 8:10–11.) Christ is therefore a living person and presence, someone whom people can "know" (Phil 3:8, 10). This presence is particularly experienced for Paul when believers gather together for worship, community discernment, and celebration of the "Lord's supper" (1 Cor 10:15–22; 11:17–34), a supper at which Jesus is both host and guest, and during which his redemptive death is recalled and his victorious return antici-

5. On this see especially Wright, *Resurrection*, 312–29.

6. In 1 Corinthians 15 Paul does not assert this point explicitly but assumes it when he argues (1 Cor 15:42–50) that the body of the believer will be transformed into an imperishable "spiritual body" and thus "bear the image of the man of heaven" (Jesus)—the same point he makes more explicitly in Phil 3:21. On this entire subject, see especially Wright, *Resurrection*, 340–56, who rightly stresses that the phrase "spiritual body" does *not* mean non-physical but rather Spirit-enlivened.

7. This is implied also by the resurrection appearances in the gospels.

pated. Christ the resurrected Lord is so present in and to the church that the church itself can be called the body of Christ (1 Corinthians 12).

It should not surprise us, therefore, that Paul's most basic understanding of believing existence, individually and corporately, is summarized in his frequently used phrase "in Christ," or "in the Messiah" (e.g., Rom 6:11; 8:1; 1 Cor 1:2; 2 Cor 5:17; Gal 3:26–28). This refers simultaneously to life together in community ("in the church") and to life in vital relationship to the living Lord. This Lord is someone who can be loved (1 Cor 16:22) and served (Rom 15:18; 16:18; Col 3:24). He is to be obeyed as our Lord, even as he was obedient to the Father (Phil 2:8); he is someone who can shape the mind, energize the spirit, empower the will, and guide behavior.

The notion of a present Lord is not the same as the popular, often sentimental, idea of "what a friend we have in Jesus," for the resurrection means above all Jesus' exalted, royal status. In Rom 1:3–4 Paul writes, possibly quoting an early creed, that the gospel is about "our Lord Jesus Christ" who was "descended from David according to the flesh and was declared to be Son of God with power according to the spirit of holiness by resurrection from the dead." The cluster of titles for Jesus that we find here is very significant. Most Jews believed that the Messiah (Christ) would be a royal figure, a descendant of King David. Since kings in Israel, and in the Ancient Near East generally, were honored as sons of God, calling the Messiah the son of David is already implicitly naming him "son of God"—though still a human being. Paul tells us, however, that the resurrection is the moment at which Jesus is revealed not only as the human messianic descendant of David, but also as the Son of God in a unique way: someone who shares in the reign of God and is therefore also worthy of the title "Lord."

Thus the title "Son of God" used here and elsewhere in Paul's letters affirms Jesus' messiahship but also says much more. The Father–Son relationship is not merely a relationship between God and a royal descendant of David, for *this* royal descendant of David has not only an historical, human lineage that makes him a "son of God" but also, and much more importantly, a unique, permanent relationship with God the Father that pre-dates his resurrection, his death, and his birth. This aspect of Jesus' divine sonship is known as his "pre-existence," meaning that before what we now call the "incarnation," he was in relationship with God the Father, sharing somehow in the divine identity and activity. Thus Paul says, though without always using the language of sonship, that the pre-existent Christ had the "form" of God (Phil 2:6),[8] was the agent of creation (1 Cor 8:6), was present with the Israelites in the desert (1 Cor 10:4, 9), and then was born of a woman (Gal 4:4). But this, once again, was more than simply a human birth; it was, from one perspective, God's sending of the pre-existent Son into the world (Gal 4:4–5; Rom 8:3; cf. Rom 8:32) and, from another perspective, the voluntary self-emptying of the same pre-existent One (Phil 2:6–8; cf. 2 Cor 8:9).[9]

8. That is, participated in the divine reality; cf. 2 Cor 4:4, where Christ is the "image of God."

9. From both perspectives, the mission of the Father and the Son was our salvation, so Paul often connects "Son [of God]" language with his death and our redemption (Rom 5:10; 8:3, 32; Gal 2:20; 4:4).

The resurrection of Jesus confirms, then, that he is indeed the Messiah of Israel, but the Messiah understood as the pre-existent Son sent into the world, who is now both recognized and enthroned as such. Jesus is now "at the right hand of God" (Rom 8:34; Eph 1:20; Col 3:1)[10] and reigns as God's Son/Messiah (1 Cor 15:23–28). The title that most fully expresses that royal reality is drawn from texts like Psalm 2 and Psalm 110: "Lord." "Jesus is Lord" is at once the simplest, the most common, and the most profound confession of faith found in the Pauline letters (Rom 10:9; 1 Cor 12:3; Phil 2:11), as we noted in chapter 4. But what does this confession mean?

Jesus is Lord

What we call "religion" and "politics" have at least one thing in common—each is about loyalty. In the modern and postmodern worlds we have tried in vain to separate these two inseparable dimensions of human life. The ancients, as we have already said, knew better.

In Paul's day there were many lords and gods, as he himself acknowledges (1 Cor 8:5), but there were essentially three lords, and three corresponding gospels, vying for his loyalty and that of others. Each of these gospels was "theopolitical" in character, and each lord required devotion and loyalty that

10. In the Scriptures of Israel, God's right hand is a metaphor, drawn from the royal practice of having a vice regent who sat on the king's right, for divine rule, might, victory, salvation, protection, and even creation. According to Ps 110:1, YHWH (*kyrios* in Greek) has invited "my lord" (also *kyrios*) to sit at his right hand. The early church interpreted this as a reference to Jesus' exaltation by God the Father (e.g., Matt 26:64; Acts 2:33–34; Heb 1:3, 13).

expressed itself not only in "private" matters but also in public life.

One gospel proclaimed that the God of Israel (YHWH) is lord, or *kyrios* in Greek, the language of the Roman world into which the Hebrew Scriptures had been translated for dissemination everywhere. Paul, of course, believed that good news as a Jew, both before and after his conversion and call. Another gospel proclaimed that the emperor is lord—*kyrios*. Inscriptions and literary texts bear witness to the world's acclamation of Caesar's birth, accession to power, salvation, and justice as "good news." And yet a third gospel proclaimed that Jesus is lord—*kyrios*. This was a gospel that offended both Jews and Romans, for it ascribed to a crucified criminal the honor due to YHWH or Caesar alone.

Paul and other early Christians obviously believed the third of these gospels: Jesus is Lord! This acclamation looks like an early Christian motto, or confession; it appears in Paul's poetry (Phil 2:11), and in his discussion of early Christian public events such as worship (1 Cor 12:3) and entrance into the church (Rom 10:9). It is assumed elsewhere, whenever Jesus is called "the Lord Jesus [Christ]" (69 times in Paul's letters), and wherever Paul speaks of obedience or conformity to Jesus, as disciples to their master.

If Jesus is Lord, Caesar is not. The imperial claims of peace (the famous *pax Romana*), justice, salvation, and universal rule—through violence, domination, and deterrence-by-crucifixion as needed—could not be true if the one who had freely emptied out his life in obedience to God and love for others is now the lord of all. *His* peace, justice, and salvation did not look like those offered by the emperor; the two were mutually exclusive. One could not and cannot pledge ultimate allegiance to Jesus and to Caesar. This should radically call into question any understanding of Paul (based narrowly, for example, on a traditional reading of Rom 13:1–7) as politically uninterested, uninteresting, or conservative.

But if the Christian gospel and the imperial gospel are mutually exclusive, it should be obvious from all we have seen in Paul that the Christian gospel and the Jewish gospel are not. Paul's belief that Jesus is Lord could not be, and was not, in conflict with his conviction that YHWH is Lord. In fact, the two gospels are actually one, because they originate in and proclaim the same Lord—the God of Israel, now revealed in his Son, who as God's Son and Messiah is also appropriately designated "Lord" and given the acclamation due to God alone.

Perhaps the most astounding example of this conviction about, and devotion to, Jesus as Lord appears in the poem in Philippians (Phil 2:6–11). There Paul says not only that Jesus is Lord, but also explains the significance of this name or title: (a) it is given to him by the Father; (b) it is in fact the "name above every name," meaning the divine name YHWH; and (c) it means that Jesus can and will be given the devotion due God alone. Paul makes this last point in a particularly powerful way: by quoting one of the most potent Scriptural acclamations of Jewish monotheism—that YHWH alone is God and Savior—and applying it now to Jesus:

> [21]. . . . There is no other god besides me, a righteous God and a Savior; there is no one besides me. [22]Turn to me and be saved, all the ends of the earth! For I am God, and there is no other. [23]By myself

> I have sworn, from my mouth has gone forth in
> righteousness a word that shall not return: "To me
> every knee shall bow, every tongue shall swear." (Isa
> 45:21b–23; cf. Phil 2:9–11)

Elsewhere Paul applies other YHWH texts and attributes additional divine functions to Jesus. Two of the most important are the biblical themes of "calling on the name of the Lord" for salvation, meaning now to invoke the name of Jesus, and the "day of the Lord," the future coming of God for salvation and judgment that was announced by the prophets; it becomes for Paul the *parousia* and "day" of Jesus.[11]

It is very important to note, however, that Paul is not merely claiming that God has shared some divine duties with the human Jesus. Rather, Paul is saying that Jesus shares in the divine functions and properly receives divine devotion because he shares the divine identity. In fact, Paul displays this conviction by showing how he has reinterpreted the most basic Jewish monotheistic affirmation, known as the *shema* (Hebrew for "hear"): "Hear, O Israel: The LORD [Greek *kyrios*] is our God [Greek *theos*], the LORD alone. You shall love the LORD your God with all your heart. . . ." (Deut 6:4–5). Paul concurs that "there is no God but one" (1 Cor 8:4), but in Paul's hands, the central claim of this text becomes "for us there is one God [*theos*], the Father, from whom are all things and for whom we exist, and one Lord [*kyrios*], Jesus Christ, through whom are all things and through whom we exist" (1

---

11. On the first of these two themes, see Joel 2:32, used by Paul in Rom 10:13 and 1 Cor 1:2. On the second, see, for example, Isa 13:6–11; Joel 1:15; 2:1, 31; 3:14; Amos 5:18–20; and Mal 4:5; and then 1 Cor 1:8; 5:5; 16:22; Phil 1:6, 10; 1 Thess 5:2. (Specifically on judgment, compare Rom 14:10 and 2 Cor 5:10.)

Cor 8:6). Throughout Paul's letters, we see this divine union and yet distinction between God (the Father) and Jesus (the Son and Lord).

By reinterpreting Israel's monotheism in this way, Paul is either committing blasphemy, morphing monotheism into ditheism, or expressing a new understanding of Jewish monotheism—what some have called "christological mono-theism," that is, monotheism that includes Jesus Christ as Son and Lord within the identity of God.[12] The last of these options would have been the only remotely possible option for a faithful Jew, and it is the best understanding of Paul's convictions—convictions that almost certainly predate him in the early Jesus-as-Messiah movement.[13]

The Resurrection and the Human Condition: Now and Later

Such is the meaning of Christ's resurrection for God and for Christ himself—Christ the Son of God and Lord. But what does that mean for us? We may sketch a few salient points that will be further developed in later chapters.

---

12. When Paul refers to Christ as the image of God, he appears also to equate Christ's "glory" (splendor) with the glory of God (2 Cor 4:4–6).

13. The scholarly work on the complex topic of "christological monotheism" is vast. On the whole subject, see Fee, *Pauline Christology*. For the attribution of YHWH texts to Jesus, see especially Capes, *Yahweh Texts*. On early Christian devotion to Jesus, see Hurtado, *Lord Jesus Christ*. And for the NT's inclusion of Jesus in the identity of God, with special reference to the cross, see Bauckham, *God Crucified*. The term "christological monotheism" is appropriate as far as it goes but is ultimately inadequate because it fails to take into account the presence of the Spirit in Paul's understanding of God (see chapter 6).

(1) To begin with, the resurrection of Jesus is itself also something in which we can participate, first of all existentially ("newness of life" now; Rom 6:4)[14] and then also physically ("a resurrection like his" later; Rom 6:5, 8): In Romans 6 Paul seems to draw metaphorically on the language of death and resurrection to depict the end of one way of life and the beginning of a radically new way of living. But Paul's language is more than metaphorical; he is speaking about participation in the activity and story of God that centers on Jesus' resurrection. In fact, in a very important sense, believers' present resurrection is bodily, because it involves the re-orientation of bodily existence away from Sin and self and toward God and righteousness. Thus we may say that believers' present resurrection *in* the body anticipates their future resurrection *of* the body.

This is one of the reasons bodily resurrection—both Christ's and ours—is so important to Paul. It is a fundamental and non-negotiable building block of his ethic. It has been said that without the resurrection, Christianity collapses. For Paul, that is certainly true, but it is especially true for his view of how believers ought to live. The body is the means by which we encounter others and serve God. The believer's new life in the body consists of the offering of one's body and its various "members" to God as a spiritual sacrifice, like a priest to a deity (Rom 12:1–2), and as an act of obedience, like a slave to a master (Rom 6:11–13). It is because the body was created by God, has been "purchased" by God in the act of redemption (Christ's cross), and will one day be resurrected

14. Cf. Col 3:11–13; Eph 2:1–6.

by God that Paul can pronounce every bodily deed as a matter of grave spiritual significance (1 Cor 6:12–20).

If Christ's "resurrection" and ours were simply about the survival of the soul or something similar, then what one does to and with the body would matter much less, if at all. However, because Christ's resurrection was a resurrection and transformation of his embodied self, and because our resurrection will likewise be a resurrection and transformation of our embodied selves, what we do with and to our bodies has tremendous, even eternal, significance. What ties these two types and times of resurrection together, then, is their shared bodily character and the reality of *transformation*—moral transformation of life in the body now, and actual transformation of the body in the future. These two kinds of resurrection correspond also to Christ's defeat, by his cross and resurrection, of our two greatest enemies, Sin and Death, that is, our liberation from Sin now and from Death later (Romans 6). This liberation involves, once again, our bodies—how we use them now, and what their final destiny is later. Thus neither neglect nor indulgence of our bodies—or any part of the created order—is an appropriate manifestation of belief in the resurrection and its corollary, the redemption of the cosmos (see chapter 12).

(2) Secondly, believers have God's resurrection power available to them in the presence of the Spirit of God (Rom 8:10–11; Eph 1:19–20). The Spirit powerfully enables us to discern, desire, and do the will of God. But, because the Spirit is the Spirit of the Father and the Son, resurrection power takes the form of the cross. Just as the resurrection validates and vindicates the cross, so also the resurrection empowers believers

to embody the cross ourselves, and it validates such embodiment, or cruciform existence, as the mark of the presence of God in a person or community.

(3) Thirdly, affirming that the resurrected Jesus is Lord makes a theopolitical claim on our loyalty. When we confess Jesus' lordship, we acknowledge the God of Israel, now most fully revealed in his Son, as the rightful sovereign of our personal and public lives, the only one to whom ultimate love, loyalty, and obedience are due. It is simultaneously a rejection, therefore, of other ultimate claims on our lives, whether religious, political, or ideological (those emanating from various "-isms").

To confess "Jesus is Lord," as we have seen, means that we obey him. This master, however, is the incarnation of perfect divine love, so that obedience is not a burden but a joy; in fact, it is—paradoxically—freedom. The humiliated one has been exalted; the obedient one is now to be obeyed (Phil 2:8, 12[15]); the crucified one is now present in the community by the Spirit, making such obedience both desirable and feasible for all (Phil 2:1, 13). Because it is Jesus Christ *crucified* whom we confess as Lord, our lives will become conformed to the "mind of Christ" displayed in his self-emptying, self-giving incarnation and death (see chapter 11).

(4) Finally, when we acknowledge that God has raised Jesus from the dead, we confess that the story of Jesus really is the story of God. We see in his story the definitive activity of God

---

15. The Greek text of Phil 2:12 says "obeyed"; the NRSV erroneously adds "me" (Paul) after the verb.

in the world. We can summarize that basic story of Christ in Paul's letters in the following way:

> pre-existence → sending/self-emptying → humilia-
> tion/death → resurrection → exaltation/enthrone-
> ment → reign → return

The events of death and resurrection have inaugurated the new age, so we find ourselves now living in the new age under the lordship of the exalted Jesus. (As we saw in chapter 5, the fullness of that new age awaits the return of Jesus.) This is the true master story of God and now also of humanity.

Summary

We have seen in this chapter that at the heart of Paul's message is his conviction that God raised Jesus from the dead, which means both that Jesus is Messiah, Son of God, and Lord and that we who acknowledge him as such share in his new life now and will also later share in his bodily resurrection from the dead. To confess Jesus as Lord is to pledge ultimate allegiance to him as sovereign. To fully participate in Christ's death, resurrection, and lordship is the raison d'être of all humanity. It begins with dying and rising with Christ, the subject of the next chapter.

Reflection

1. Returning to the question raised at the beginning of the chapter, Why does the resurrection matter so much?

2. Some have suggested that the waning of Christian conviction about the resurrection of Christ in the modern era has negatively affected our understanding of Christian disci-

pleship generally and of faith, love, and hope in particular. What are those effects, and how can they be undone? How *should* the resurrection impact the Christian life?

3. How might the confession of Jesus as Lord challenge (a) the loyalties and priorities of contemporary Christian individuals and churches generally and (b), more particularly, the attitudes and practices that merge Christian faith and nationalism ("civil religion")?

9

"Justified by Faith . . . Crucified with Christ"

Reconciliation with God through Participation in Christ

✼ In the 1930s, as much of the Christian church in Germany was starting down the road to compromise, extreme nationalism, and complicity with the Nazis, Dietrich Bonhoeffer wrote prophetically about cheap grace and its antithesis, costly grace. "Cheap grace," he proclaimed in the first sentence of his famous book *The Cost of Discipleship*, "is the deadly enemy of our Church."[1] It is "the justification of sin without the justification of the sinner"; it is "grace without discipleship, grace without the cross, grace without Jesus Christ, living and incarnate." It is "the grace we bestow on ourselves."[2] Costly grace, on the other hand, is "the pearl of great price . . . the kingly rule of Christ . . . the call of Jesus Christ at which the disciple leaves his nets and follows him. . . . Such grace is *costly*

---

1. Bonhoeffer, *Cost of Discipleship*, 45. The original German title was simply *Discipleship* (German *Nachfolge*), and a new English translation retains that title. All quotations here, however, are from the more widely known translation; italics are in the original.

2. Ibid., 46.

because it calls us to follow, and it is *grace* because it calls us to follow *Jesus Christ*."[3]

Today, once again, many Christians and churches face the temptations of cultural captivity, "spirituality" without discipleship or ethics, and knee-jerk nationalism. These are all forms of cheap grace, or cheap justification—a relationship with God in which God is believed to be a kind of cosmic agent of "salvation" (happiness, blessing, security, prosperity, etc.) who requires little or nothing of the allegedly "saved" or "blessed." Cheap justification is justification without transformation, without conversion, without justice. Once again, someone needs to speak, not merely of grace, but of *costly* grace; not merely of justification by faith, but of *costly* justification by faith.[4] That someone is Paul.

What is at Stake?

In Romans 5:1 Paul writes, "Therefore, since we are justified by faith, we have peace with God through our Lord Jesus Christ." Justification by faith is commonly thought to be the hallmark, even the center, of Paul's theology—his signature theological dish, so to speak. If this is true, or even if justification is only a very important part of Paul's theology, rather than the center, we need to get it right. Yet many interpretations of justification in Paul are foreign to the full scope of the apostle's thinking, reflecting a later urge on the part of

3. Ibid., 47.

4. Or, more precisely, "justification by grace through faith." ("Salvation" language occasionally replaces "justification," as in Eph 2:8–10.)

Protestants to distinguish themselves from Catholics by stressing "faith" over against "works."[5]

Some interpreters of Paul have objected to the claim that justification is the center of Paul's theology, since it receives extended discussion in only two letters, Galatians and Romans. They say that something like "participation in Christ"—especially dying and rising with him and living "in" him (themes we have tasted in previous chapters)—has that place in the apostle's experience and thinking. If this is true, then we must still figure out what justification is, and how it relates to participation in Christ.

A growing number of readers of Paul want to hold these two candidates for the Pauline center together, and that is the view to be explored in this chapter.[6] First, we will define justification. Then, we will see what Paul means by faith, and thus justification by faith. This investigation will take us to passages in Paul that, ironically, speak of participation in Christ. That is, Paul himself keeps together what many of his readers have split apart. Our goal is to discover their inseparability, and its importance.

5. Bonhoeffer's sharp point on this subject (*Cost of Discipleship*, 59) is worth noting: "The word of cheap grace has been the ruin of more Christians than any commandment of works."

6. One of the first to do so in recent times was E. P. Sanders in his influential book *Paul and Palestinian Judaism*. Although other aspects of this book have been rightly challenged, and although Sanders does not offer a fully satisfying account of the connection between justification and participation, he was on the right track.

Justified: Reconciled to God

The word "justification" refers to one of several important but frequently misunderstood dimensions of Paul's thought about, and experience of, the relationship between humans and God. Most people would probably say it has something to do with salvation, or with going to heaven based on faith (believing that Jesus died for our sins) rather than works (doing good deeds and thereby earning God's approval). It is not difficult to find texts in Paul that can be used to support this interpretation (e.g., Rom 3:20–24; 4:3–4, 23–25), even if they say nothing at all about "going to heaven." Despite the apparent face value of such texts, justification is more complicated than—and in fact radically different from—the common perception of its meaning.

The word "justification" and its siblings (just, justice, etc.) translate families of Hebrew and Greek words that may also be rendered into English by terms like "righteousness" and its relatives (righteous, etc.). Some Bible translations prefer one set of terms, some the other. In either case, Paul's understanding of justification/righteousness stems from several interlocking streams of biblical thought:

- the conviction that the God of the covenant is just/righteous;

- the corollary expectation that God's covenant people will be just/righteous;

- the conviction that God's righteousness expresses itself in salvific, transformative action for the covenant people and for all creation;

- the image of the just/righteous God judging the people, like a judge in a courtroom, both now and on the future day of judgment; and

- the vindication of the just/righteous on that day.[7]

What does all this mean for Paul? Historically, interpreters of Paul have had two main understandings of justification in Paul. On the one hand, some (mostly Protestants) have said it means that righteousness is *imputed* to those who believe in Christ. It is a divine pronouncement or verdict, based on the merits (death) of Christ. On the other hand, some (mostly Catholics) have said that it means righteousness is *imparted* to those who believe in Christ. It is a divine action that actually transforms the one who believes. Although some recent Catholic-Protestant conversations and statements have brought these two views closer together, they represent at least two different emphases.[8]

The traditional Protestant definition sees justification as a divine *declaration*, stressing the stream of law-court imagery noted above, while the other view sees justification as a divine *transformation*, stressing the covenantal and ethical streams. Since Protestant Christians tend to think and talk more about justification than do their Catholic (or Orthodox) counterparts, the most common Christian understanding of justification is indebted to law-court imagery. In fact, that imagery is often articulated as a legal fiction: because of Christ, God the

7. For a similar view of the convergence of images, see Wright, *What Saint Paul Really Said*, 113–19, and Bird, *Saving Righteousness*.

8. See especially *The Joint Declaration on the Doctrine of Justification*, issued by Catholics and Lutherans in 1999 and available in various published and online formats.

judge *counts* people as righteous even though they are not. Although there may be some truth in this, it can be a dangerous belief that leads to cheap justification and cheap grace.

More recently, the so-called "new perspective" on Paul has generally rejected the traditional understandings of justification, especially the Protestant version, as too focused on the individual and God. ("How can I, a sinner, be justified before a holy God?") The new perspective understands justification in Paul as *covenant membership*, or membership in the people of God (i.e., Israel) without the requirement of doing the works of the law. The "doctrine" of justification in this view is really a statement about the inclusion of Gentiles (who don't have to become Jewish to become Christ-followers), and "doing the works of the law" is understood, not as keeping the commandments, but as observing Jewish identity markers such as circumcision, diet, and calendar. Some critics have accused this perspective of throwing out the proverbial baby with the bath water.[9]

In response to these contrasting views, we may offer the following definition of justification as one that captures elements of both traditional interpretations but also places a more appropriately Pauline accent on the *covenantal* and *corporate* dimension of justification/righteousness:

> *Justification is the establishment of right covenantal relations—fidelity to God and love for neighbor—by means of God's grace in Christ's death and our co-crucifixion with him. Justification therefore means co-resurrection with Christ to new life within the people*

9. Among many books about the new perspective, see especially recent ones by a chief proponent—Dunn, *New Perspective*—and a chief critic—Westerholm, *Perspectives Old and New*.

> *of God now and the certain hope of acquittal, and thus*
> *resurrection to eternal life, on the day of judgment.*

Justification, then, is about reconciliation, covenant, community, resurrection, and life.[10] And this reality is brought about by death—Christ's death *for us* in the past and our death *with him* in the present, all due to God's initiative and grace.

Paul indicates the meaning of justification as reconciliation by making the two realities parallel in one of his most famous texts on justification, Rom 5:1–11, the beginning of which we cited above:

> [1]Therefore, since we are <u>justified</u> by faith, we have peace with God through our Lord Jesus Christ, [2]through whom we have obtained access to this grace in which we stand; and we boast in our hope of sharing the glory of God. . . . [10]For if while we were enemies, we were <u>reconciled</u> to God through the death of his Son, much more surely, having been <u>reconciled</u>, will we be saved by his life. [11]But more than that, we even boast in God through our Lord Jesus Christ, through whom we have now received <u>reconciliation</u>. (underlining added)

We would be mistaken, however, to think that this "peace with God" is some bed of roses, some version of "cheap" justification. The verses omitted in the passage from Romans 5 quoted above tell us that the experience of faith, love, and

---

10. This breadth of meaning to the notion of justification is also echoed in the parable of the Good Samaritan (Luke 10:25–37), where questions of life, covenant-keeping, and justification appear. Michael Bird (*Saving Righteousness*, 4) defines justification as "the act whereby God creates a new people, with a new status, in a new covenant, as a foretaste of the new age."

hope is tempered by the reality of suffering, which for Paul is one of the natural consequences of life with God in Christ. Furthermore, Rom 5:1–11, about justification by God's grace as reconciliation, is soon followed by Romans 6, about baptism as co-crucifixion and co-resurrection with Christ. As we will see below, the two experiences are actually one and the same, viewed from different perspectives. And if justification, which for Paul is an event of God's grace, means co-crucifixion and co-resurrection with Christ (which is also an event of God's grace), it can hardly be understood as "cheap" grace. "The gospel Paul preaches deals not merely with forgiveness but with *transformation*."[11]

Paul's understanding of justification as reconciliation means that a narrow, "judicial" (sometimes called "juridical" or "forensic") view of justification as a divine declaration and legal fiction is simply inadequate, for in Scripture what God declares, God effects—in this case, restoration through forgiveness. Equally inadequate is the similar view of justification in accounting terms (see Rom 4:1–12 and the language of righteousness being "reckoned" or "credited"). Despite the origin of this language in Scripture (Gen 15:6, about Abraham), and despite its clear importance to Paul, this is not all that Paul says about justification. In fact, for Paul the fact that the God in whom Abraham believes is the promise-keeping One who brings life out of death, implying that justification is a kind of resurrection from the dead, is a crucial part of what makes Abraham's justifying faith exemplary (Rom 4:16–25). Judicial views wrongly privilege one aspect of justification, or one metaphor for it (the legal), while ignoring others, including

11. Hays, *Moral Vision*, 38.

the extended description that Paul himself provides in Rom 5:1–11. Justification as reconciliation means that justification is about a two-way relationship, and when the Bible speaks about the relationship between God and people, it does so in the two idioms of covenant and life, as we will see below.

We must also remember that justification is about justice, also understood as a relational reality. Paul says that his gospel reveals the justice of God (Rom 1:17, 3:21), God's *dikaiosynē*—a phrase often translated "the righteousness of God." We can certainly retain the noun "righteousness," but if we do, we should probably exchange the related verb "to justify" for something like "to rightwise," "to set right," or even "to make righteous." However, these are all a bit awkward, and they are subject to quite individualistic interpretation. So we probably do better to keep the verb "justify" and use the noun phrase "justice of God"—understood as God's *saving* and *restorative* justice—to remind us of the close connection between justification and justice. Moreover, "the (saving) justice of God" reminds us also that Paul is saying that the gospel is about a special kind of divine character trait and activity—*God's* justice—that is in some sense parallel to but radically different from other kinds of justice, such as Roman justice or American justice.[12]

Roman justice was a way of bringing order out of chaos, but it resulted in a system of more justice for some (the elite) and less for others. Furthermore, it required a system of punishment and deterrence that included the shame of public crucifixion for those who threatened the order that Roman

---

12. It is also important to note that "the justice of God" does *not* mean God's punitive justice.

justice created. In other words, like the justice of Phinehas, the violently zealous Israelite who was likely Paul's role model,[13] Roman justice required the exclusion and even the destruction of anyone perceived to be a threat to the peace/the social order/justice. The descendants of Roman justice, including certain contemporary versions of domestic as well as international justice, inevitably follow a similar pattern, culminating in the destruction of the enemy.

This brings us back to the discussion of Paul's conversion in chapter 2. Relying on the example of Phinehas, Paul believed that his zealous, even violent, activity—allegedly for the honor of God and the good of Israel—would result in his justification.

The saving, restorative justice of God revealed in the gospel is an alternative way of setting people right with God and with one another. It takes place not by inflicting violence on the enemy, but by absorbing violence on behalf of the enemy. Its extreme *modus operandi* is not to crucify but to *be* crucified. It does not require the destruction of the enemy but the embrace of the enemy.[14] The justice of God, therefore, is not the opposite of compassion but the very expression of compassion. It is at once the manifestation of God's *faithfulness*, because this is the way God is, and of God's *grace*, because it is not what humans deserve. Romans 3:21–26 and especially 5:6–8 demonstrate that Christ crucified displays this kind of divine justice, simultaneously revealing that "normal" forms of justice are in fact alien to the gospel:

13. See the discussion in chapter two.
14. See Volf, *Exclusion and Embrace*.

> [6]For while we were still weak, at the right time Christ died for the ungodly. [7]Indeed, rarely will anyone die for a righteous person—though perhaps for a good person someone might actually dare to die. [8]But God proves his love for us in that while we still were sinners Christ died for us. (Rom 5:6–8)

Those who are embraced by such grace-filled justice cannot remain loyal to alien forms of justice, for imperial justice and cruciform, restorative justice are incompatible; God's forgiveness transforms us. "For our sake he [God] made him [Christ] to be sin who knew no sin, so that in him we might become the righteousness [justice] of God" (2 Cor 5:21). The gospel requires and empowers its beneficiaries to become God's ambassadors (2 Cor 5:17–21), to practice the justice of forgiveness, reconciliation, and restoration rather than the justice of shock and awe. The various versions of the Truth and Reconciliation Commission, first employed in post-apartheid South Africa under the leadership of Archbishop Desmond Tutu, are perhaps the most dramatic theopolitical manifestations of God's kind of justice in recent history.

Invading other nations or oppressing minorities within domestic or disputed territories displays a justice alien to the restorative justice of the cruciform God. Excluding people of other nations, races, or languages displays a justice alien to God's righteousness. Retaliating for mistreatment by a superior or spouse or friend displays a justice alien to God's mode of justification. That is why Paul's gospel requires—and enables!—the transformation of people from their natural Phinehas-like and Rome-like tendencies to the grace of reconciliation and embrace.

In Paul's Bible, as we noted in chapter 2, there were two possible paths to justification through divine "reckoning" ("X was reckoned to him as righteousness"). The path of Phinehas is the way of justification by works taken to its logical extreme: by zeal, self-righteousness, and lethal violence. Those who follow this path are erroneously confident of their own righteousness and justice, even while dealing in death and committing injustices against others (see Rom 2:1—3:20). It is a path that leads to exclusion and destruction. It is justification by the self. The path of Abraham, on the other hand, is the way of justification by faith: by trust, by forgiveness, and by life—by resurrection from the dead. It is justification by God. Those who follow this path are sure only of God's goodness and faithfulness. It is a path that leads to inclusion and restoration (Rom 4:9–17; Galatians 2; Ephesians 2).

The legacy of Phinehas lives today in the hearts and minds of people, non-Christian and Christian alike, who think that self-righteous zeal—always aggressive and sometimes murderously violent, as in the case of suicide bombers and other indiscriminate killers—is their calling in history and will be their justification before God. To such misguided people—and to those of us who simply think we can merit God's favor or take grace for granted—Paul offers a robust alternative: justification by faith.

Co-Crucified: Sharing the Faith of Jesus

We have had to strip away inadequate understandings of justification. Not surprisingly, conventional understandings of "faith" do not measure up to Paul's view either.

If we asked "people on the street" to define faith, we would receive a variety of answers. Among these might be "trust," especially trust in something unseen, or perhaps "conviction," especially conviction in spite of evidence to the contrary. To "lose faith" is to lose confidence, whether in a person, a relationship, a dream, an impersonal entity like a corporation or a government, or God.

Faith is a complex human experience, and Paul preserves this complexity while giving it a unique twist. While affirming its character as trust and conviction, Paul connects faith to the experience of Jesus as God's faithful Son. Faith is more than trust; it is also fidelity, or loyalty.

At root, this is actually not unique to Paul; it is a very Scriptural and Jewish understanding of faith or trust as inclusive of loyalty. Israel's call to know and trust the one true God was simultaneously a call to *pledge allegiance* to God, and to demonstrate that allegiance through a life of covenant loyalty. Scripturally speaking, faith and obedience are two sides of one coin.

So too with Paul. He bookends his letter to the Romans with a summary of his mission, which is to bring about "the obedience of faith" among the Gentiles (Rom 1:5; 15:18; 16:26). At the same time, his gospel addresses the reality of disobedient Israel (Rom 11:30). Thus Paul affirms humanity's universal disobedience, and he affirms that it has been undone by the obedience of one representative human—the Messiah Jesus (Rom 5:19). Although Jesus' fidelity to God manifested itself throughout his life, Paul finds its quintessential expression in his obedience "to the point of death—even death on a cross" (Phil 2:8).

As noted in chapters 4 and 7, recent scholarship has suggested that there are several passages in Paul where a phrase that used to be translated "faith in Jesus Christ" (or Jesus/Christ/the Son of God) should be translated "the faith of Jesus Christ."[15] In these texts, Jesus' death on the cross is described as his act of faith, or faithfulness—his loyalty to God. Elsewhere, Paul calls Jesus' faithfulness his act of righteousness and/or obedience (Rom 5:18–19; Phil 2:8).

Justification, it is clear from Paul's letters, comes to those who acknowledge the death and resurrection of Jesus on their behalf. But Paul does not see this positive response to the gospel of Christ's death and resurrection—that is, he does not see "faith"—merely as an intellectual affirmation or even simply as an act of trust in the efficacy of those events. Rather, Paul sees faith as a *sharing* in the death of Jesus that is so real, so vivid, that it can be described as being crucified with Christ, or co-crucified (Rom 6:6; Gal 2:19). This was the reality that grasped Bonhoeffer, too: "When Christ bids a man, he bids him come and die."[16]

When Paul describes justification in Gal 2:15–21, one of his most important treatments of the subject, he says that it has (1) an *objective* basis in the faithful death by crucifixion of Jesus and (2) a *subjective*, or *existential*, basis in the believer's co-crucifixion with him. That is the essence of faith—dying to an old existence characterized by disobedience to God through complete identification with the obedience of Jesus. Paul both defines this complete identification with Jesus' death (co-crucifixion) as faith and states that it occurs in

15. Rom 3:22, 26; Gal 2:16 (twice), 20; Gal 3:22; Phil 3:9.

16. Bonhoeffer, *Cost of Discipleship*, 99.

the public expression of that faith known as baptism (Rom 6:1–11). Moreover—and this is crucially important—the act of co-crucifixion is not a matter of human effort; it is a graced response. Paul expresses this both in Galatians and in Romans by using the passive voice—the "divine passive," as it is called: "[we] were baptized into his death . . . we have been united with him in a death like his . . . our old self was crucified with him" (Rom 6:3–6); and "I have been crucified with Christ" (Gal 2:19). Ultimately, God (through the activity of the Spirit—see Gal 3:1–5) is the agent even of our own participation in the death of Jesus.

As we noted in chapter 7, Paul views Jesus' death on the cross not only as the ultimate expression of his fidelity to God, but also as the definitive manifestation of his love for humanity—for us. In one act of faith and love, therefore, Jesus embodied the two tables of the law, loyalty to God and love for neighbor, thus performing the quintessential act of covenant fulfillment. As such, the death of Jesus is the means of our justification when we participate in it through co-crucifixion by faith and baptism. To share in that death is to identify with its covenant-fulfilling quality and to become part of the new covenant community that re-enacts Christ's covenantal loyalty and love day by day. Hence justification is a communal reality in several respects, and the discussion of it here is a preface to subsequent chapters, as we have already suggested.

The act of identifying with, and participating in, Christ's death is only half the story, however, for the gospel is about death followed by resurrection. Although Christ's death is necessary for our justification, Paul also says that "Christ was raised for our justification" (Rom 4:25); his resurrection to life effects our resurrection to new life. Those who share in Christ's death also share in his resurrection, such that an old self dies and a new one is raised (Rom 6:4–11). We are raised to "newness of life" (Rom 6:4), the life of obedience or covenant loyalty and of love, a life of right relations with both God and others. Paul calls this "living to God" (Rom 6:10–11; Gal 2:19), and argues forcefully that it is inaugurated not by our own efforts, or by possessing traditional marks of membership in the covenant people (such as circumcision), or by misguided zeal (like that of Phinehas, and of Saul/Paul before Damascus), but only by Christ's gracious death and our participation in it. Justification by faith, then, is another way of saying life to God through death to self, or life with God through death with Christ. It is the ultimate paradox: life comes through death, both Christ's and ours. Justification is by co-crucifixion, a work of God's grace.

Reconciliation with God, then, is by God's own initiative, or faithfulness, expressed in the faithfulness of Jesus, to which we respond by sharing in that faithful death in the act of saying "yes" to God and expressing that "yes" in baptism.

Occupied: In Christ and Christ Within

Paul describes his converts at Corinth as those who were "washed . . . sanctified . . . [and] justified [i.e., by God] in the name of the Lord Jesus Christ and in the Spirit of our God" (1 Cor 6:11). This Trinitarian description of their experience suggests that participation in the very life of God is at the core of Paul's gospel and mission. As we saw in chapter six, already in his earliest letter Paul speaks of a relationship with God the Father; God's Son, the Lord Jesus; and the Holy Spirit (1 Thess 1:1–10).

Paul's creative way of describing this participatory experience of God is by using the image of mutual indwelling, or reciprocal residence—especially believers being in Christ and Christ (or the Spirit of Christ, or of God) being in, or among, believers.[17] The believer is now incorporated, not into a dead Messiah, but into the resurrected Christ. At the same time, paradoxically, the living Christ "moves in," taking up residence in the believer. "It is no longer I who live, but it is Christ who lives in me" (Gal 2:20), Paul says, representing all believers. The co-crucified "I" lives again by the power and presence of the living Christ.[18]

That is, believers are "occupied"—taken over and inhabited by the Spirit of God/Christ, in whom they, in turn, live.[19] To say that believers live in the Spirit of Christ is to say that they inhabit the three-in-one cruciform God.[20]

It should be emphatically noted at the outset that this experience is not that of a private mystic but an experience shared in community. To be sure, Christ lives within the individual believer, but Christ dwells also in the community of believers assembled in his name. Similarly, for Paul an individual

17. See especially Rom 8:9–11 for the most concise example of mutual relationship. Paul usually uses "in" language to connect believers to Christ or the Spirit, but "in God the [or "our"] Father and the Lord Jesus Christ" occurs in 1 Thess 1:1 and 2:2.

18. Although Paul does not explicitly use the word "resurrection" in Galatians 2, the experience he describes is clearly resurrection to new life.

19. Although Paul does not use terms like "reciprocal residence" or "occupied," the basic notion is clearly there (e.g., Phil 3:12).

20. On this subject, see further my forthcoming book *Inhabiting the Cruciform God*.

believer lives in Christ, but he or she does so only by being in the concrete body of Christ—the Christian community. We in the West would more readily grasp this reality if we lived in a less individualistic culture, a "we" culture rather than a "me" culture. We would also see it more clearly if we remembered that "Christ" means 'Messiah," and to be "in" Christ is to be "in" the Messiah, who is for Paul the one descendant, or seed (NRSV "offspring"), of Abraham (see Gal 3:16, 27–29) and thus the individual who embodies the covenant people of God. To be in him is to be in the covenant people. And the reality of people being in Christ means the start of the prophetically promised new creation (2 Cor 5:17).

The person who says "yes" to the gospel and is justified by co-crucifixion with Christ in the experience of faith and baptism makes a spiritual and sociological move from being outside Christ and the covenant people of God to being inside Christ and God's people. Using what is sometimes called "transfer language," Paul can speak of "believing into Christ" (the literal meaning of a key phrase in Gal 2:16) or being baptized into Christ (Rom 6:3; Gal 3:27). More vividly, he calls this being clothed with Christ (Gal 3:27), an experience that must be renewed day by day (Rom 13:14). Christ envelops the individual and the community that lives in him, beginning a long-term process of shaping both believers and churches into his image (Rom 8:29; 2 Cor 3:18), a process also of having the mind of Christ within (Phil 2:5).

To be in Christ/in the Spirit is, therefore, also to have Christ/the Spirit within. The idea of the indwelling of God's Spirit within people and communities comes from the prophets, especially Ezekiel (Ezek 11:17–20; 36:22–32; 37:1–27).

The purpose of this indwelling is to enable God's people to live, to be resurrected to new life in order to know and do the will of God—to keep covenant with God as God's holy people. In other words—to be reconciled and justified.

In Paul's experience of God as Father, Son, and Spirit, focused on the events of cross and resurrection, this reality of divine indwelling works itself out in a very peculiar and interesting way. As noted above, the Spirit given to believers is both the Spirit of the Father and the Spirit of the Son. Because the Spirit who dwells in believers is the Spirit of the One (God the Father) who raised Jesus from the dead, believers have God's resurrection power available to them (Rom 8:10–11). This is the power of new life, of transformation. At the same time, because the Spirit given to them is the Spirit of the crucified Jesus, the Son (Gal 4:6; cf. Gal 2:20), resurrection power takes the form of the cross; it is *cruciform* resurrection power. Just as the resurrection validates, vindicates, and completes the cross, so also the resurrection empowers us to embody that cross. *The living Christ of the resurrection is the loyal and loving Christ of the cross; the living one who dwells within is the faithful and loving one who gave himself in obedience to God and in love for us.* This is the essential claim of Gal 2:20, and the heart of Paul's cruciform spirituality: "It is no longer I who live, but it is Christ who lives in me. And the life I now live in the flesh I live by the faithfulness of the Son of God, who loved me by giving himself for me" (my translation).

For Paul Christ crucified and resurrected is both the external mold and the internal dynamism of Christian existence. Christian "ethics," which we will explore in the next chapter, is therefore simply the ongoing expression of the life of Christ through those in whom he dwells and who dwell in him. We have already hinted at this reality in our discussion of the connection between justification and justice. Or, to describe that life more completely, Christian ethics is the resurrection power of the justifying, cruciform, three-in-one God expressing itself as the sign of the cross in daily life. It is the life of living in and for this God and of becoming more and more like this God who lives within—a process the Eastern churches have called *theosis*, or divinization. It is nothing other than justification properly understood as the restoration of our covenantal relationship with God and of the image of God (known in Christ) within us and, therefore, of becoming God-like, or holy.

Summary

To summarize: justification and participation are two sides of the same coin, the coin of relationship to God in Christ by the Spirit, because faith for Paul is above all sharing in the faithfulness of Jesus that culminated on the cross. The experience of justification-participation is intensely personal but not private or individual; we are justified, we are baptized, and we participate in Christ in the context of a community and in relation to a wider world. That is, in justification-participation we are reconnected not only to God in Christ by the working of the Spirit, but also to other people. That truth will lead us to the next chapter on community life in Christ. Justification-participation is a simultaneously "spiritual" and "ethical" reality. Our covenantal connection to others places ethical responsibilities on us, such as the tasks of justice and inclusion.

There is no such thing as cheap justification for Paul. As Ephesians puts it, salvation is *by* grace but *for* good works (Eph 2:8–10). The two are inseparable.

Reflection

1. When and where have you observed the phenomenon of "cheap justification"? Why is it so attractive to us?

2. How have you typically defined faith? How does Paul's understanding of faith force us to reconsider some of our operating definitions?

3. How does the understanding of justification presented in this chapter challenge versions of salvation/justification with which you are familiar?

4. What does it mean to "participate" in Christ?

10

"Called to be Saints"

Countercultural, Multicultural
Community in the Spirit

✣ The word "saints" often connotes a small, special class of super-holy people who are recognized, officially or unofficially, for what average people might hope to attain but never will. That is not what Paul means when he uses the Greek word that is translated "saints" or "holy ones"—*hagioi*. What Paul has in mind is a group of diverse people who have been apprehended by the resurrected crucified Messiah—justified, crucified, and occupied—and who live together as a distinctive, even countercultural, community in him.[1] "Saint," in other words, is the title for every believer in Christ, and "saints" is the designation of every community in Christ. In this chapter, then, we are looking at some features of what Paul calls the church (another misunderstood term), or assembly (Greek *ekklēsia*), which is the countercultural, multicultural community of those justified by God through Christ's cross and living in Christ by the indwelling power of the Spirit.[2]

1. "Countercultural" describes a group, within a larger culture, possessing key beliefs and practices that are deliberately distinct from the larger culture.

2. See further the relevant chapters in *Holiness and Ecclesiology*, ed. Brower and Johnson.

The Renewed People of God:
A Called, Set-Apart Assembly

Behind Paul's understanding of the church are two realities that come together in his vision. The first is the assembly (Hebrew *qahal*) of Israel. Israel had been chosen and called by God to be a people set apart, distinct from her neighbors in belief and behavior, a people fully dedicated to YHWH. "You shall be holy for I am holy" was God's word to Israel, connecting the divine character to the nation's calling (Lev 11:45; 19:2, etc.; cf. Exodus 19). When the people assembled, priests, psalmists, and prophets (when they were faithful) reminded them of God's distinctive character and of their peculiar calling.

The second reality that Paul engages is the assembly (Greek *ekklēsia*) of the Greco-Roman city (Greek *polis*). The *ekklēsia* was something like the city council, a group of male elders who met to deliberate about local issues and to ensure that the *polis* was faithful to its heritage and values. The *ekklēsia* had the additional duty—especially if the *polis* happened to be a Roman colony and/or home to the imperial cult (e.g., Corinth, Philippi, Thessalonica, Ephesus)—of dutifully and creatively expressing its loyalty to Rome and to its lord and savior, the reigning emperor.

Paul uses the term *ekklēsia* for "the church" as a term of both continuity and discontinuity. On the one hand, it designates the assembly of believers who affirm Jesus as Lord and constitute the renewed "Israel of God" (Gal 6:16). On the other hand, this assembly exists as an alternative *ekklēsia* and even an alternative *polis*, since it incorporates not just a few leaders but an entire believing community. It exists as a counterculture to embody the values of its true savior and lord, Jesus the crucified and resurrected Messiah.

The church, therefore, is a visible, even a "political" reality, rather than just a group with invisible "spiritual" bonds, whose mission it is to be a living commentary on the gospel it professes, the story of the Lord (Jesus) in whom the church exists and who lives within the assembly. (See especially Phil 2:1–15.) As such, the church reflects the character of the God revealed in Christ. This is what "holiness" and "sainthood" mean for Paul. This countercultural community is not produced by human effort, nor does it occur to perfection overnight; it is a process of divine activity and communal and personal transformation (e.g., Rom 12:1–2; 1 Thess 3:11–13; 5:23–28). To be holy is to be different, different from those outside the church and different from the way we used to be, changed from what was "then" to what is "now" (Gal 4:8–9; 1 Cor 6:9–11; Eph 2:1–6; Col 3:1–7).

Some Images of the Assembly

Such an assembly of God's people in Christ is depicted in a variety of ways in Paul's letters. Its visible, public, theopolitical character is expressed in the foundational word *ekklēsia* discussed above. Similar theopolitical language can be found in the famous image of the church as the body of Christ (1 Corinthians 12), the human body having served previous thinkers, such as Aristotle, as an image of community—the "body politic." For Paul, "body" language expresses several realities of life in Christ: the intimate connection of believers to Christ himself (see also 1 Cor 6:12–20); the interdependency of believers together in worship and mission; the unity-in-diversity that happens, or should happen, because of varied gifts and cultures within the assembly (see also Rom 14:1— 15:12; Ephesians 2–3); and the radically un-Roman preferential option for the weaker members of the body. The "body of Christ" also suggests the presence of Christ in the world—in and through the body of believers.

Another image of the church in Paul's letters suggesting presence is the temple, a term that would resonate with Jews but also with Gentiles. Paul uses the image in 1 Cor 3:16 (where "you" is plural, meaning "you all, together"), stressing the holiness of the temple as well as the consequences of defiling it by destroying its peace and unity. Similar language appears in Eph 2:11–22, where the emphasis falls on the unity of Gentiles and Jews in Christ. The image of a "dividing wall" (Eph 2:14) between Gentiles and Jews, now dismantled in Christ like the Berlin Wall, alludes to the prohibition of Gentiles from entering the central areas of the Jewish temple in Jerusalem.

Unity in Christ is a persistent Pauline theme, expressed in several ways, but most famously in the text of Gal 3:28: "There is no longer Jew or Greek, there is no longer slave or free, there is no longer male and female; for all of you are one in Christ Jesus" (cf. Col 3:11). This is central to Paul's understanding of the church as a multicultural community—his version of Dr. Martin Luther King's "beloved community," where differences of race, ethnicity, class, and gender do not divide but unite in the love of God. This does not happen automatically, even in Christ. The reality of Gal 3:28 does not erase cultural differences, nor does it guarantee that sinful human beings will always display the unity they have in Christ. In fact, Paul composed his longest and most important letter,

Romans, with the theme of "Gentile and Jew" and with the goal of uniting Roman believers from diverse cultural backgrounds who were more disposed to mutual critique than mutual acceptance (see especially Rom 14:1—15:13). Paul also sought to unite Gentile and Jew, East and West, more broadly by allowing the assemblies in Rome to participate in his collection for the impoverished churches in Jerusalem. To this day, Christians around the world struggle to accept and manifest their cultural diversity (black-white, North-South, East-West, etc.) as unity and to prevent bias and prejudice from infecting the beloved community.

This image of a diverse yet unified community is closely related, in turn, to yet another image of the church, that of a family of adopted brothers and sisters who are heirs together of all God's riches in Christ. We see this first of all in Paul's frequent usage of the term "brothers [and sisters]" to address his communities.[3] We see it also in the way Paul understands believers as descendants, or children, of Abraham by faith, and thus also as children of God (Gal 3:23–29). Paul capitalizes on the Roman practice of adoption to express the reality that this status of becoming God's children is due to a special act of divine fatherly grace, the result of which is full access to the father's inheritance—that is, sharing with the elder Son, Jesus, in the future glory of the Father (Rom 8:12–17). Because *all* members are adopted into this family, all are equal: male and female, Jew and Gentile, black and white, European and Latino/a, etc. The church is an alternative family, what sociologists call a "fictive family," one constituted not by sharing in the blood of biological parents but in the blood of Jesus.

3. The Pauline letters have about seventy instances of believers being addressed as "brothers," meaning "brothers and sisters" (so NRSV).

To Paul, of course, the church is actually the most real of all families, with the one true Father beneficently providing for all—the very thing the emperor claimed to be and to do. The church is both alternative *polis* and alternative family. Thus we have come full circle; the theopolitical and the familial images are really two sides of the same coin.

Life Together

These realities of the church's life in the world—as assembly, body, temple, and family—suggest the purposes it accomplishes when it meets together and when it lives in the world from meeting to meeting. We get glimpses of this in brief texts in several letters (e.g., 1 Thess 5:11–22), but we get the most detail in 1 Corinthians.

First of all, the assembly meets to worship God. In that context it both *hears from God*, through prophecy and teaching, and *speaks to God* in praise, prayer, and hymn-singing. (See 1 Corinthians 14 and Colossians 3). Secondly, the assembly also meets to speak to one another. The assembled brothers and sisters encourage and admonish one another (1 Cor 5:1–13; 1 Thess 4:18; 5:11). They seek to discern God's will (Rom 12:1–2), display the mind of Christ (Phil 2:1–5), and do the bidding of the Spirit—all made possible by their having the three-in-one God present with them as they come together. It is this God who is active among them (1 Cor 12:1–3; Phil 2:12), and their coming together is an expression of their mutual indwelling with Christ and the Spirit. They express this union especially in their Spirit-inspired prayers, as they address God together, brothers and sisters in the Lord Jesus, as "Abba"—the Aramaic word "Father" that Jesus also used (Rom 8:15; Gal 4:6).

Both in speech from and speech to God, and in speech to one another, the assembly especially recites its foundational stories and considers how they can best embody those stories in their life together in the world. These foundational stories include the Scriptures (i.e., the Old Testament); the creed about the saving acts of God in Christ's death and resurrection (1 Cor 15:1–8) or incarnation, death, and exaltation (Phil 2:6–11); brief narrative summaries focusing on the significance of Jesus' death (Gal 1:4; Rom 3:21–26); and narratives of Jesus' instituting the Lord's supper (1 Cor 11:17–34).[4] The assembled believers hear the story and discern the mind of Christ. Guided by the Spirit, plus the words of Scripture, tradition, and Paul, they look together for God's specific call to them to be a countercultural community of people infused with the Spirit of Christ, a Christophany—a manifestation of Christ—in and for the world.[5]

The role of reciting the foundational narratives in the Pauline assemblies can therefore hardly be overestimated. Yet these *recited* narratives were also accompanied by *enacted* narratives, or symbolic rituals, that served to inaugurate people into Christ and then to sustain them in him. The enacted narrative of baptism brought cleansing and the establishment of right covenant relations to the believer who experienced it upon profession of faith in the gospel. The act transferred him or her out of the realm of sin and into the realm of Christ through a complete identification with his death, burial, and resurrection.[6] (This is reflected in narratives focusing on the

4. See examples in chapter 4.

5. Harrisville speaks similarly of believers as an "epiphany" of Christ (*Fracture*, 113–24).

6. For the sociological significance of baptism and other rituals in the Pauline churches, see Meeks, *First Urban Christians*.

existential significance of participating in Christ's narrated experience; see Rom 6:1–11; 1 Cor 6:11.) The old self and its ways died, and a new self was born—a resurrection to new life now in anticipation of a resurrection of the body later.

After baptism, the enacted narrative of a meal together hosted by the Lord Jesus recalled for the assembly the past, present, and future significance of Jesus' salvific death.[7] The "Lord's supper" (1 Cor 11:20) is the Lord's because he is the host and because those present have an experience of communion (solidarity and sharing—Greek *koinōnia*; see 1 Cor 10:16–17) with him and with one another together in him. This meal is the enacted narrative, or sacrament (to use a later term), of bifocal existence in Christ, bringing the community together to experience once again the cross in light of the *parousia*, the crucified one as the coming one (1 Cor 11:26), and to make sure that their life together in him in the present reflects the reality of their Lord's past and their Lord's future. To the degree that it does not, transformation is needed.

Although Paul's focus in 1 Corinthians is clearly on the integrity of the church's internal relationships—specifically its care for the poor and weak (1 Cor 11:22)—there can be no artificial line between the call for God's kind of cruciform justice in the community and a witness to God's same justice in and for the wider world. Paul himself calls the church to live in love and peace with "all"—including those outside the community, even enemies (Rom 12:9–21; Gal 6:10; 1 Thess 5:15). The how and why of that kind of witness is discovered

7. Although direct evidence for what Paul calls "the Lord's supper" appears only in 1 Corinthians, it is likely that he passed on this tradition, inherited from the practice of other early churches, to all the churches he founded, drawing attention to it at Corinth only because it had become a scandalous practice there.

in the solidarity with Christ and others that the Lord's supper both permits and requires. Their imaginations spurred on by this experience of amazing grace, members of the body of Christ can then instantiate, or embody, the love and justice of God wherever they are, being willing to suffer with and for a suffering world.[8] (See also Rom 8:18–27.) That is sainthood, or holiness, in action.

Holiness, however, is not for Paul a product of human effort; it is the "fruit of the Spirit"—the *Holy* Spirit.

Walking in the Spirit

As we saw in the previous chapter, life in Christ is also life in the Spirit—the Spirit of God, the Spirit of Christ, the Holy Spirit. As with Christ and believers, the relationship is mutual: in the Spirit and the Spirit within (e.g., Rom 8:9). All Christian existence is charismatic existence—infused with the presence, power, fruit, and gifts of the Spirit.[9] The role of the Spirit in the Pauline communities was essential to their life together, a life depicted, in traditional biblical language, as "walking" in the Spirit (Gal 5:16)—an image unfortunately lost in many modern translations that render "walk" as "live."

For Paul the Spirit relates us first of all to God the Father, being the expression and assurance of God's love (Rom 5:5)

8. In one of the communion rites in the United Methodist Church, the minister prays, "Make them [the gifts of bread and wine] be for us the body and blood of Christ, that we may be for the world the body of Christ, redeemed by his blood." As the body of Christ, the church extends the justice of God in Christ beyond its walls, especially to the poor and weak.

9. The term "charismatic" comes from the Greek word *charisma*, meaning "a gift [of grace—Greek *charis*]." Although it is often associated with those who experience such gifts as speaking in tongues, I use it here to describe a Spirit-filled life more generally.

and the impetus for our exclaiming "Abba, Father!' (Rom 8:15; Gal 4:6). The Spirit, like Christ, also intercedes for us before the Father and prays when we cannot (Rom 8:26–27). Moreover, the presence of the Spirit makes us, as both individuals and assemblies in Christ, sacred temples of God (1 Cor 3:16; 6:19).

The Spirit, in a word, brings life and holiness (Rom 8:1–13). The Spirit brings life as the Spirit of the One who raised Jesus from the dead,[10] and since this life is the covenantal, countercultural life expected of God's people, it is a life of holiness (1 Thess 4:7). The Spirit makes it possible for us to fulfill the demands of a covenantal relationship with God (Rom 8:3–4). The Spirit is thus the personal, animating power and presence of God—the One who guides and molds the church (Rom 8:13–14; Gal 5:18, 25) in the power of the resurrection.

Since the Spirit of God, as we have seen, is simultaneously the Spirit of Christ, the Spirit's resurrection power manifests itself in the shape of the cross of Jesus the Lord. The Spirit therefore also relates us to Christ, leading us to confess that "Jesus is Lord" (1 Cor 12:3) and transforming us into the image of Christ (2 Cor 3:18). (We will explore that reality in some detail in the next chapter.) Moreover, as James Dunn suggests, it was the palpable experience of life in the Spirit, relating Paul and his churches to the Father and the Son, that gave rise to Paul's reflections on the character and activity of God that would later be called Trinitarian theology (see also chapter 6).[11]

---

10. Rom 8:11; cf. Eph 3:20; Col 1:11; 2:12.

11. Dunn, *Theology*, 264.

The Spirit is also the source of what Paul calls both "fruit" (singular) and "gifts" (plural). The fruit of the Spirit is the multidimensional, godly, Christlike character (Gal 5:22–26) expected of and offered to all in Christ. The gifts are distributed as the Spirit wills for the activity (ministry) and growth of the body (1 Corinthians 12; Rom 12:4–9; Eph 4:1–16). Although everyone receives a gift, not all gifts are given to all.[12] Since there is one and only one Spirit, the Spirit creates unity in diversity, whether that is diversity of gifts (1 Corinthians 12) or of cultures, socioeconomic status, and gender (Gal 3:28). This unity is called "sharing" (NRSV), "solidarity," or "fellowship" (Greek *koinōnia*) in the Spirit (Phil 2:1). Believers' responsibility is to cooperate with the Spirit's unifying activity (Gal 5:13–16; Eph 4:1–6; Phil 2:1–4).

We must note at this point that the Spirit's work of inclusion and unification always occurs in concert with the work of sanctification. That is, the Spirit of unity is simultaneously the Spirit of holiness, and one aspect of the Spirit's activity does not happen without the other. In practical terms, this means that Christian unity and inclusion have limits because the gospel calls people to transformation, and the Spirit makes that transformation possible (1 Cor 6:9–11). Those who persist in practices that violate the gospel are not to be welcomed in perpetuity but dismissed from the assembly for the good of the community as well as the individual (1 Cor 5:1–13). As harsh and intolerant as that may sound, especially to Western ears, it is the logical consequence of understanding the church as a *holy* or *countercultural* community. The trick,

12. We may claim that we have been given the gift of administration rather than speaking in tongues, but we may not claim that we have the fruit of peace rather than self-control.

as most churches know, is defining the practices that must be excluded, and it is often easier not to deal with the issues but rather to dispense with holiness in the quest for unity.

Nonetheless, the church must learn to deal with controversial issues such as sexuality. Although holiness is in no sense restricted to sexual purity, the churches Paul founded, rooted in Judaism, constituted a sexual counterculture—even if they sometimes failed to live up to their calling fully. The theme of sexual holiness appears, for example, in Paul's earliest letter (1 Thess 4:3–8) and in what many would call his most practical letter, 1 Corinthians. In that letter he reminds the Corinthians that their conversion involved changes in sexual behavior (1 Cor 6:9–11), and he urges them to view sexual matters, like everything else, with one eye on the cross and resurrection and the other on the *parousia* (1 Corinthians 5–7).

Walking in the Spirit, then, is another way of saying that we participate already, between the first and second comings, in the new creation God has begun in Christ. That new creation, as we have seen, is not yet fully here (and perhaps ongoing church disputes bear the most poignant witness to that truth), so Paul employs vivid images to express the reality of the experience of the Spirit: the Spirit is God's "seal on us" (mark of ownership) and the "first installment," "pledge," or "guarantee" of our redemption—the reality of God's saving life, but not yet the fullness of that reality (2 Cor 1:22; 5:5; Eph 1:13–14; 4:30).

Summary

The church is God's countercultural (holy) and multicultural beloved community that walks in the Spirit of Christ the

Lord. This community is shaped by the foundational narratives about Christ, both recited in the community and enacted by the power of the Spirit, as it exists together as a living exposition of those narratives.

At the center of those narratives is the cross of Christ. Holiness—the fruit of the Holy Spirit, the work of God—is ultimately a Christophany, a manifestation of Christ to the world.[13] And the only Christ Paul knows, the Christ who is both the power of and the paradigm for Christian existence, is Christ *crucified*. Ultimately, life in the church, in the Spirit, is about conformity to Christ crucified—to which we now turn.

Reflection

1. How does Paul's understanding of the church compare with your prior understanding of the church and with popular images of the church today more generally?

2. Many people believe that it is possible, and perhaps even preferable, to be a Christian without participating in the life of a church. How would Paul respond to this sentiment?

3. Contemporary Christian experience of the Spirit seems to swing between the extremes of (a) dullness that borders on non-experience and (b) overly zealous hyperactivity. How might Paul's experience of the Spirit address this situation?

13. Moreover, since we have seen (chapter 7) that the cross is in fact the ultimate *theophany*, the church properly living in the Spirit is actually a theophany.

11

"Conformed to the Image of God's Son"

Cruciform Faith, Hope, and Love

Holiness for Paul, we have suggested, is a countercultural life shaped by the presence of the crucified and resurrected Christ who is present within his people. But what does that mean concretely?

The "Science of the Cross"

Edith Stein (1891–1942) was a German Jewish philosopher who came to Christian faith by reading the autobiography of Teresa of Avila (1515–1582); she was baptized on New Year's Day in 1922. She taught in a Dominican college and opposed Nazi anti-Semitism even as her career, and eventually her life, was threatened by the power she resisted. In 1933 she joined a Carmelite community of religious sisters and was given the name Teresia Benedicta a Cruce: Teresa Blessed by the Cross.[1] In late 1938 Edith fled to a Carmelite community in Holland, but in 1942 the Nazis arrested her, like many other Christians of Jewish heritage, and sent her to die as a martyr at Auschwitz.

1. This was in recognition of her spiritual debt to Teresa of Avila and John of the Cross, who had worked with Teresa to reform the sixteenth-century Carmelite orders of nuns and monks.

Edith Stein embraced a spirituality that she called *Kreuzeswissenschaft*—German for the "science of the cross." It was a paradoxical spirituality of love in the face of hate, joy in the midst of darkness and suffering, resurrection in times of crucifixion. In English, a corresponding term that has been coined in reference to Paul's own experience and teaching is "cruciformity," or conformity to the crucified Christ.[2] This noun derives from the more common adjective "cruciform," meaning cross-shaped, applied first, literally, to churches built in the shape of a cross and then, metaphorically, to the lived experience of individuals and communities that bear witness to the cross by being patterned after Christ's self-giving, loving death as God's suffering servant.

Cruciformity Defined

"Cruciformity" is not a term that appears as such in Paul's letters. (Nor does the more common adjective "cruciform.") It is a term invented to capture a crucial dimension of Paul's experience and thought. So what is it?

We noted earlier that many people associate Christ's cross with the *source* of their salvation, and perhaps even as something they must "take up." But many people have never thought of the cross in connection with the very *shape* of their salvation—that is, the form of their life, either individually or corporately—their spirituality. Cruciformity is cross-shaped existence in Christ. It is letting the cross be the shape, as well as the source, of life in Christ. It is *participating in* and *embodying* the cross. It may also be described, more technically, as non-identical repetition, by the power of the Spirit, of the

2. For a complete discussion, see Gorman, *Cruciformity*.

narrative of Christ's self-giving faith and love that was quint-essentially expressed in his incarnation and death on the cross. It is, therefore, a *narrative* spirituality, a spirituality that tells a story, the story of Christ crucified.

Cruciformity is Paul's all-encompassing spirituality. It is the *modus operandi* of life in Christ. It is fellowship, or commu-nion, with the Lord Jesus (1 Cor 10:16–17), sharing the "mind of Christ" (Phil 2:5; 1 Cor 2:16), and conformity to the image of God's Son (Rom 8:29; 2 Cor 3:18; cf. Phil 2:5–11), which is a process of conformity to his death (Phil 3:10). This con-formity is not merely a conformity to his suffering—though it includes that (e.g., Rom 8:17; Phil 3:10)—but conformity to his cross-shaped narrative more broadly, the narrative of self-giving loyal obedience to God (faith) and self-giving love of neighbor. It is thus a life of ongoing co-crucifixion with Christ (Gal 2:19–20) that, paradoxically, is life-giving, both to those who live it and to those affected by it. Cruciformity begins at the time of faith and baptism, when the old self is crucified with Christ and dies, and a new self rises.

In the previous chapter we noted that because the Spirit is the Spirit of the One who raised Jesus from the dead, be-lievers have God's resurrection power available to them. Yet, because the Spirit is also the Spirit of the Son, resurrection power takes the form of the cross; it is *cruciform* power. Just as the resurrection validates and vindicates the cross, so also the resurrection empowers believers to embody the cross them-selves and validates cruciform existence as the manifestation of the life of God in a community or individual. Ironically and paradoxically, therefore, the new life to which the self rises in faith and baptism is life in the shape of the cross!

We have already discussed the initial process of dying and rising (chapter nine) that inaugurates cruciform existence in Christ. We will discuss cruciform faith, love, and hope momentarily. But first we consider some aspects of the larger framework of cruciformity.

The Structure of Cruciformity

To live in Christ is to have a "bifocal" existence, as we characterized it in chapter 5. This means that as we live in the overlap of the present age and the age-to-come, we keep our eyes focused backwards on Christ's cross and resurrection and ahead to his *parousia* (return). It also means that as we live in the remnants of the old age (of injustice, etc.), we do so *according to the cross*, in the hope that evil will be resolved *by God* in the future. Our living cannot violate the nonviolent, self-giving, God-obeying love of the cross, which determines the structure and fabric of our existence day by day. This means that the experience of dying and rising carries forward from baptism into daily life; each day, each moment becomes an occasion for expressing the resurrection power of God through cross-shaped decisions and actions. This can only take place for Paul by the ongoing work of the Spirit in our lives—the work of transformation out of the mindset of this age and into the mind of Christ (Rom 12:1–2; Phil 2:5). What is that mind?

One of the most famous lines in all of Paul's letters is the phrase "whenever I am weak, then I am strong" (2 Cor 12:10). This is not merely the paradoxical musing of a profound spiritual writer, though it is that. It is above all an existential claim grounded in a theological conviction: the foundational knowledge that Christ crucified is the power of God (1 Cor 1:18–25), as we saw in chapter 7. That is, weakness, *as humans measure power and weakness*, is the way God is and the way God operates in the world. To live in a way that corresponds to this reality may indeed be paradoxical, but above all it is faithful; it is *true*. To seek power as humans measure it—with wealth, control of others, prestige, physical might—is not merely to make a mistake; *it is to betray and renounce the gospel*. It is important therefore to note that Paul does not understand the gospel as power *and* weakness but as power *in* weakness. God works in and through the nobodies and the nothings of this world (1 Cor 1:18–31)—from Christ crucified to simple believers confident in the presence of Christ's cruciform power in their lives. This clearly does not mean, however, that Paul endorses the oppression of the weak by the powerful; rather, it is his way of affirming the biblical theme that God's ways are not our ways and that "blessed are the meek" (Matt 5:5).

The cruciform principle of "power in weakness" provides the context for understanding similar motifs in Paul's letters. One of these is the theme of joy in suffering. Cruciformity is not primarily about suffering—it is about covenantal loyalty and love that sometimes (often?) *result in* suffering, as they did for Jesus. Thus suffering, though not synonymous with cruciformity, is a constitutive element of it.

Suffering most certainly marked Paul's life. As we saw in chapter 2, he catalogs his sufferings on several occasions; their frequency and scope are quite breathtaking. Paul sees these sufferings as part of his participation in the Messiah's sufferings (2 Cor 1:5; Rom 8:17; cf. Col 1:24) and in the suffering of the entire cosmos before the birth of the new creation (Rom 8:18–28).

Many of Paul's churches also experienced suffering as a result of their faith in Jesus. Paul was relieved when he heard they were surviving and even thriving in the midst of persecution (e.g., 1 Thess 3:1–10). He taught them that they should not be surprised by suffering, that it was normal (1 Thess 2:14–16; 3:1–5; Rom 8:18–39), and that it did not signify the absence and displeasure of God but rather the presence and love of God, even as Christ's suffering death was the manifestation of God's presence and love (Rom 8:28–39). In fact, suffering was something to rejoice in. Was Paul a masochist? A sadist? No.

Paul himself experienced joy in suffering. He counted it a privilege, a grace, to share in Christ's sufferings, and he told his churches that they should, too (Phil 1:29). Why? As with Christ's suffering, Paul saw good emerge from his own suffering (see further below), and he rejoiced at that, even when he was imprisoned. Paul's letter to the Philippians, written from jail, is full of joy; in fact the "joy" word-family appears a dozen times in the letter. Paul's own experience gave him the authority to write to the Roman believers that they should even boast, or exult, in their suffering, which produces character, endurance, and eventually hope (Rom 5:1–5). So this does not reveal a disorder in Paul's personality or perspective. Rather, it reveals his deep conviction that Christ's suffering and death constituted a revelation of divine love for the world, a love into which he and his churches were now caught up; they were called to narrate to the world, in word and deed, the suffering and reconciling love of God in Christ. To suffer for others is to absorb evil and pain rather than inflict them; that was God's way in Christ, and it became Paul's way, too, the natural consequence of his conversion from violence as his means to justification before God (see chapter 2).

So, if Paul is not a masochist, neither is the God he sees revealed in Christ's cross. Indeed, for Paul suffering is also a prelude to glory, as crucifixion is to resurrection; shame gives way to honor in the economy of God. Just as Christ was humiliated and then exalted, in the pattern of the suffering servant of Isa 52:13—53:12, so also those who suffer with him as God's servants will be glorified with him (Rom 8:17; Phil 3:10–11). Paul even employs unusual terms to designate this overarching pattern of participation in Christ: to co-suffer and to be co-glorified (Rom 8:17; Greek *sympaschomen* and *syndoxasthōmen*).[3]

The cruciform principle of power in weakness also provides the framework for Paul's experience and theology of life in death. The sufferings and other self-giving actions of apostles and everyday believers alike have life-giving effects on others, just as Jesus' death for us brought about our justification, our new life with God. Paul states this most eloquently perhaps in 2 Cor 4:7–12, which says in part, "We are afflicted in every way, but not crushed; perplexed, but not driven to despair; persecuted, but not forsaken; struck down, but not destroyed; always carrying in the body the death of Jesus, so that the life of Jesus may also be made visible in our bodies" (vv. 8–10).

---

3. For a thorough discussion of Paul and suffering, see Jervis, *At the Heart of the Gospel.*

As we look at the structure of cruciformity, we see a unified life lived according to the cross. But it is possible also to identify three aspects of it that Paul calls faith, hope, and love.

"Faith, Hope, and Love Abide"

Perhaps the most well-known text from Paul's letters is 1 Corinthians 13, cherished as a "hymn to love" that nearly everyone has heard at weddings. Ironically, in its original context that chapter of 1 Corinthians has absolutely nothing to do with marriage, yet its closing words about faith, hope, and love do provide a succinct summary of life in Christ according to Paul. Historically faith, hope, and love have been called the "theological virtues." They "abide" (1 Cor 13:13). We may refer to them also as the Pauline triad.

This triad appears several times in Paul's letters with the same three Greek words, though not in the list form we find in 1 Corinthians 13,[4] and other times with slight variations. What do these three terms mean for Paul? First, they are the "stuff" of justification. Note the definition of justification we offered in chapter 9, and the appearance of the three italicized terms that correspond to faith, hope, and love:

> Justification is the establishment of right covenantal relations—*fidelity* to God and *love* for neighbor—by means of God's grace in Christ's death and our co-crucifixion with him. Justification therefore means co-resurrection with Christ to new life within the people of God now and the certain *hope* of acquit-

4. See also 1 Thess 1:3; 5:8; Gal 5:5–6.

tal, and thus resurrection to eternal life, on the day
of judgment.

Second, and not surprisingly, these three realities—as we have
already seen—are all intimately connected to Paul's unique
focus on Christ crucified. Faith, hope, and love are *cruciform*
faith, hope, and love.

For Paul, faith and hope are two aspects of our relationship with God, while love is primarily oriented toward other
people. Cruciform faith and hope, coupled with cruciform
love, correspond to the two great biblical, covenantal obligations to love God and neighbor: the "vertical" and the "horizontal" dimensions of covenant. We will look first at faith
toward God, then consider love toward others, and finally
return to hope toward God.

Faith as Participation

Our English verbs "believe" and "trust," plus the nouns
"belief" and trust" as well as the nouns "faith" and "faithfulness," which lack a corresponding English verb, are all possible translations of words that are members of a single Greek
word-family (*pistis, pisteuō*). Forms of this word-family appear in Paul's letters more than 200 times. Depending on the
context, Paul can stress one aspect or another of this complex
phenomenon that we will refer to as faith.

Sometimes Paul seems to lay heavy emphasis on the af-
fective dimension of faith (trust), while at other times he seems
to understand faith more intellectually, as a deep conviction.
Yet in both cases, faith for Paul is something that cannot remain simply in the heart or head; it is a verb of action, an act
of faithfulness and thus obedience. As we noted in chapter 9,

Paul even characterizes his mission as working to bring about the "obedience of faith" among the Gentiles (Rom 1:5; 16:26). When one believes or disbelieves the gospel and God (Rom 10:6–11, 14, 17), one also obeys or disobeys (Rom 10:16, 21), because the good news is not merely a divine announcement or promise; it is a call, a summons. To believe and confess that Jesus is Lord is hardly just an intellectual affirmation; it is a personal and public commitment to *obey* this Lord Jesus; it is a promise of loyalty, a pledge of allegiance. Faith is not something that happens once; it is the ongoing reality of life in Christ.

Faith, then, for Paul, is the appropriate and total human response to God and the gospel. It is trust, conviction, obedience, and loyalty. The "faith" word-group is Paul's vehicle for expressing what other biblical writers would call the "love" of God—our trust, devotion, fidelity. Although Paul occasionally speaks of love for God (Rom 8:28; 1 Cor 2:9; 8:3), his basic terms for our relationship with God come from the "faith" word-family.

Paul's use of the faith word-group for this purpose, and his understanding of it as obedience/faithfulness as well as trust and conviction, is rooted in the Old Testament and in Jesus. It is a *covenantal*, or relational, notion of faith. Paul highlights one important aspect of this when he speaks of Abraham's trust in the promise of God, rooted in his conviction that God brings life out of death (Rom 4:9–25). Abraham is a prototype of Christian faith because he trusted the promise of God to do precisely that (in the case of his barren wife Sarah)—the same kind of promise fulfilled in the death and resurrection of Christ.

In the Old Testament, however, love for God is not merely an emotion or conviction; it is loyalty to God and the ways of God (see, e.g., Deut 6:4–25). Love or faith toward God (as devotion, trust, and/or conviction) is inseparable from faithfulness (service, obedience, loyalty). So too with Jesus, whose death as God's Servant and beloved Son is characterized by Paul as his ultimate act of obedience (Rom 5:19; Phil 2:8) and faith/faithfulness (Gal 2:16, 20; 3:22; Rom 3:22, 26; Phil 3:9).[5] Jesus is thus the ultimate paradigm of Christian faith, exemplifying its covenantal significance as trusting obedience, even to the point of death. Faith, as love for God, is therefore a form of servanthood, even "slavery," to God (Romans 6). Paradoxically, however, this faith is freedom—freedom from Sin and from ourselves to be what God created us to be; it is *bonded* freedom and thus *liberating* service.

But what is perhaps most unusual about Paul's experience and understanding of faith, as we remarked in chapter 9, is its participatory character. That is, the response of faith is a participation in Christ's death and resurrection—not merely obedience to or imitation of Jesus as God's faithful one but a real *sharing* in his experience (Rom 3:26)[6] and thus in him. As we have already seen, Gal 2:15–21 suggests that "justification by faith" means that Christ's faithfulness is the *objective* ground of justification and that our sharing in that faithfulness, by co-crucifixion, is the *subjective* ground of justification. Faith, then, is a death experience that leads to a resurrection experience—that is, to life, to justification.

5. See the alternative translations in the footnotes of, e.g., the NRSV, as well as the discussion in chapters 4, 7, and 9.

6. The end of Rom 3:26 should be translated "the one who has the faith of Jesus" not "the one who has faith in Jesus."

To trust in God, to acknowledge the gospel, to believe God raised Jesus from the dead, to be convinced that Jesus is Lord, to obey him, to share in his faithfulness—this is the appropriate, multidimensional human response to God's activity in Christ. It is what begins a right covenantal relationship with God ("justification"), and it is the character of daily life in that covenantal relation to God. Faith is not a one-time experience but an ongoing reality; it needs to be constantly exercised and renewed in order to remain true, living faith.

Such faith, like that of Jesus, issues in love.

Love as the Self-Expression of Faith

Like faith, love is a word people fill with all kinds of significance. For many, love is an emotion rather than an action.[7] For Paul, however, love is a verb, an action. This becomes especially clear in the Greek text of 1 Corinthians 13. Where the English translations have a series of adjectives ascribed to love ("love is patient, love is kind," etc.), the Greek text that Paul actually wrote has a string of *verbs* associated with love. The closest we can get in English is to translate them as "love *acts* patiently, love *does* kindness," etc. Like faith, then, for Paul love is an action-word, a covenantal term that describes the fundamental relationship that should exist among God's people and from God's people toward others. If faith is the essential "vertical" relationship in the covenant, love is its corollary "horizontal" relationship. Faith expresses itself in love (Gal 5:6).

7. Or if it is an action, is only a romantic or sexual action—"making love."

In Paul's letters, the shape of love is spelled out most fully in 1 Corinthians 13. Here and elsewhere in Paul we see that love has two fundamental characteristics: it does not seek its own interests (1 Cor 13:5), but it seeks the interests (meaning the good) of others (Rom 15:1–2; 1 Cor 10:24, 31–33; Phil 2:14). It is, in other words, self-emptying and self-giving. This understanding of love is rooted in Paul's story of Christ.

That story, of course, is one of self-emptying, kenotic, or cruciform love. Paul narrates it poetically in Phil 2:6–11: although [x] not [y] but [z], meaning *although* [x] one possesses a certain status, one *does not* [y] exploit it for selfish gain *but* [z] acts for the good of others. Paul adopts and adapts this narrative pattern on numerous occasions, not only to tell the story of Jesus, but also to describe his own apostolic life and to exhort others to share in the story of Jesus, too. One example of each will have to suffice. About his own ministry, Paul says:

> [7][T]hough we might have made demands as apostles of Christ . . . we were gentle among you, like a nurse tenderly caring for her own children. So deeply do we care for you that we are determined to share with you not only the gospel of God but also our own selves, because you have become very dear to us. [9]You remember our labor and toil, brothers and sisters; we worked night and day, so that we might not burden any of you while we proclaimed to you the gospel of God. (1 Thess 2:7–9).

And he invites the Philippians, in the set-up to the poem about Christ's love, as follows:

> [1]If then there is any encouragement in Christ, any
> consolation from love, any sharing in the Spirit, any
> compassion and sympathy, [2]make my joy complete:
> be of the same mind, having the same love, being
> in full accord and of one mind. [3]Do nothing from
> selfish ambition or conceit, but in humility regard
> others as better than yourselves. [4]Let each of you
> look not to your own interests, but to the interests
> of others. (Phil 2:1–4)

Paul applies the principle of cruciform love to the most mundane of situations and disputes, such as two female church leaders not getting along (Phil 4:2–3), believers taking one another to pagan courts (1 Cor 6:1–11), and "strong" believers failing to adjust eating habits that could lead weaker believers into sin (1 Cor 8:1—11:1). Regarding the last matter, Richard Hays paraphrases Paul: "Jesus was willing to die for these people . . . and you aren't even willing to modify your diet?"[8] Such others-oriented, self-giving love, grounded in Christ's love for us, is therefore ultimately grounded in God's love for us (e.g., Eph 5:1–2). It can therefore be characterized also as both giving and forgiving, for generosity and grace are inherent components of God's love in Christ and of our participation in it (2 Corinthians 8–9; Eph 4:25—5:2). That translates into concern for the *material* as well as the spiritual welfare of others (2 Corinthians 8–9).

Since that divine love is extended to all, so also must Christian love be extended to all, even if Paul focuses at times on its internal rather than external forms: "[W]henever we have an opportunity, let us work for the good of all, and es-

8. Hays, *Moral Vision*, 28.

pecially for those of the family of faith" (Gal 6:10; cf. 1 Thess 3:12; 5:15).

Furthermore, since that love is extended in Christ even to God's enemies, to those who are insurgents against the divine order, an inevitable corollary of love for Paul is non-retaliation and nonviolence. "There is not a syllable in the Pauline letters that can be cited in support of Christians employing violence."[9] This is pacifism rooted in Paul's gospel of divine love and reconciliation, and it comes into play especially when dealing with those outside the community who may persecute believers (Rom 12:14–21). But God knows—and Paul knows—that non-retaliation and peacemaking are needed within the church as well (1 Thess 5:11–15). This call to peacemaking is a summons to cruciform love, the forgetting of self-interest and the preferential treatment of others (Phil 2:1–4), especially the weaker members of the community (Rom 15:1–3).

The love of which Paul speaks, then, is not primarily a set of emotions but a set of actions, the results of a commitment to serve. Paul even uses the language of being "enslaved" to one another (Gal 5:13). Paradoxically, such love is the expression of true freedom—the freedom not to be enslaved to our selves and our own desires. Thus, as with our relationship to God (faith), love is *bonded* freedom and therefore *liberating* service.

To embody the cross of God's love in Christ is perhaps the most challenging of all spiritual disciplines, but it is also the most essential, for "if I have all faith, so as to remove

9. Ibid., 331.

mountains, but do not have love, I am nothing" (1 Cor 13:2).

Hope as the Future Tense of Faith

Hope, like faith and love, is another word that people fill with their own meaning, but it is universally future-oriented. It frequently means a wish, dream, or conviction that the future will be better than the present, or that the efforts or trials of the present will result in something positive in the future. For Paul, hope is closely connected to faith, which itself has a future dimension because the gospel has a future dimension. We might therefore say that hope is the future tense of faith.

But this hope that Paul has is not merely a wish or a dream. It is confidence grounded in the character and promise of God—God's faithfulness and integrity. It is a conviction grounded in the reality of what God has done in the past and will therefore do in the future. Hope's specific focal point is the life-giving character of God, which is revealed above all in his raising Christ from the dead; like faith, hope is trust in the promise of a faithful and life-giving God (Rom 4:16–25). Abraham, Paul's great example of faith (Romans 4), is also his great example of hope (Rom 4:18). Although Abraham obviously did not see the resurrection of Christ, he knew the same God who brings life out of death.

We will have more to say about hope in the next chapter (on Paul's "eschatology," or vision of the future), but for now we must consider a few key points. First, because hope for Paul is grounded in God's integrity, as we look to the future, we need not despair but can count on the words and promises of God—no matter how bleak the picture looks at the moment. One critical example of this in Paul's letters is his wrestling with God's election of and promises to Israel, both of which seem ineffective, and therefore perhaps annulled, as Paul sees very few fellow Jews believing the gospel of the Messiah Jesus (Romans 9–11). As he looks to the future, Paul trusts the promise and integrity of God, concluding that "all Israel will be saved" (Rom 11:26) because "the gifts and the calling of God are irrevocable" (Rom 11:29).

Second, because hope is trust in the God who brings life out of death, for Paul hope produces confidence, courage, and patient endurance even when despair, once again, might be the logical conclusion. The death this hope overcomes can be literal or figurative. Paul reminds the Thessalonians that they should not grieve the death of some in their community in the same manner as those who have no hope (1 Thess 4:13–18); perhaps he had in mind the common inscription found in ancient tombs: "I was not; I was; I am not; I care not." Death is not the end for those in Christ.

Paul also knew death-like circumstances in the midst of his life, as well as that of his churches. In his ministry, characterized by much suffering, Paul found strength in God's life-giving activity both in his own life (2 Cor 1:8–11) and in the people to whom he ministered (2 Cor 4:7–15). He sounds a note of hope in the midst of suffering because "death is at work in us, but life in you" (2 Cor 4:12).

Paul's second letter to the Corinthians especially makes it clear that hope, like faith and love, is cruciform—cross-shaped—and that it both springs from and enables participation in the paradoxically life-giving dying of Jesus. Like the story of Jesus, the story of believers is one of suffering and death now, followed by resurrection, exaltation, and glory later (Phil 3:10–11, 21). But even in the present difficulties, hope, not despair, is the experience of those in Christ.

Third, then, hope obviously has much to do with suffering. Paul can even say that we "boast" (or exult, or take pride) in our sufferings, not only in the hope of "glory" to come (Rom 5:3–5). Suffering, he says, initiates a chain of endurance, character, and hope—but only in the context of an experience of God's love manifested in Christ (Rom 8:28–39) and communicated by God's Spirit (Rom 5:5). As with joy, this does not make Paul a masochist. Rather, his experience of Christ's past death and resurrection and his anticipation of Christ's future coming (and all that that means) provide once again a bifocal framework within which he, and we, can interpret our suffering, whether it be suffering for Christ and the gospel or suffering more generally.

It is Paul's understanding of present suffering in light of God's future that is perhaps the most compelling aspect of his experience of hope. Different aspects of this understanding emerge in his various letters. Two aspects, each expressed in vivid imagery, are especially noteworthy. One stresses the temporary character of suffering: "For this slight momentary affliction is preparing us for an eternal weight of glory beyond all measure" (2 Cor 4:17; cf. Rom 8:18). The other prevents this expression of hope from becoming individualistic, fanciful wishing—or, worse, the opiate of the people. Using the metaphor of birth pangs, Paul situates our suffering within a global, even cosmic, context of suffering and of hope for relief and renewal:

> ^{19}[T]he creation waits with eager longing for the
> revealing of the children of God. . . in hope ^{21}that
> the creation itself will be set free from its bondage
> to decay and will obtain the freedom of the glory
> of the children of God. ^{22}We know that the whole
> creation has been groaning in labor pains until now;
> ^{23}and not only the creation, but we ourselves, who
> have the first fruits of the Spirit, groan inwardly
> while we wait for adoption, the redemption of our
> bodies. ^{24}For in hope we were saved. . . . (Rom
> 8:19–24)

For Paul, then, hope is grounded in the resurrection and expressed as confidence in God concerning the future of the self, the church, Israel, and the cosmos. Without the resurrection, there is no hope, only an argument for despair—or for hedonism (1 Cor 15:19, 30–32).

The Theopolitical Character of Faith, Hope, and Love

The traditional theological virtues of faith, hope, and love can seem quaint and benign, but to see them as the equivalent of a boy-scout pledge to do one's duty to God, country, and little old ladies would be to miss the point dramatically.

Paul's triad of faith, hope, and love challenges us to the core, calling us to align our loyalties, our dreams, and our affections with the gospel of God, the lordship of Jesus, and the countercultural activity of the Spirit. It calls us as individuals and as the *ekklēsia* to be transformed by the renewing of our minds (Rom 12:1–2), to be transformed into a community whose politics is distinctive. By "politics" I do not mean what is normally thought of as politics, such as party affiliation and location on the liberal-conservative spectrum, but rather our "body politic": our way of being in the real, visible, public realm.

Paul's call to faith is an alternative to the ideological assent and corollary loyalty expected of Roman citizens, or citizens of any state. Faith as loyalty to God in Christ means the recognition of no other ultimate or life-determining loyalty, for (once again), if Jesus is Lord, Caesar is not. It means participation in the powerful powerlessness of Christ crucified and thus the rejection of traditional loyalties that claim their power over us and call us to participate in *their* power, whether religious, economic, political, or military. It means living with a profound hermeneutic[10] of suspicion toward the "powers" (Col 1:16; 2:15) that surround us and manifest themselves in various persons, causes, -isms, and states claiming our allegiance.

Paul's call to hope is an alternative to the pseudo-eschatological dreams of Rome and its heirs. Through worldwide supremacy and the accumulation of luxury, Rome offered peace, power, and pleasure—all tagged as divine blessings—to those under the shadow of its eagle-like wings. But it did so only by practicing grave injustices such as invasion, enslavement, exploitation, and neglect of the poor, because it lacked a god, among its many deities, that rejected power practiced at the expense of others. Paul proclaimed such a God. He offered a present experience and a future hope with a radically different peace, power, and pleasure—the peaceful reign of God and the joy of the Spirit (Rom 14:17).

---

10. Interpretive strategy or posture.

Hope as conviction about God's good future is not passive but active. It both permits and requires activity on our part, participation in what God is doing in the present that anticipates the fullness of the kingdom that will come in the near future. This activity rooted in hope is governed by the rule of love, the law of Christ (Gal 6:2). Paul's call to love is an alternative not only to the blatant violence that dominates human relations, but also to the manipulative gift-giving and "I'll scratch your back if you'll scratch mine" mentality that permeates many human cultures. This law of Christ forbids activity in the name of God that does not correspond to the divine graciousness displayed in the faithful and loving death of Jesus, and it requires an ongoing individual and communal discernment of how to actualize the love of God in creative but faithful ways. Those in Christ must "keep in step with the Spirit" (Gal 5:25, NIV), learning how the Spirit continues to empower the faithful in a life that corresponds to the reconciling, redeeming love of God in Christ, the love that is both giving and forgiving. Reconciled and redeemed, the community re-incarnates that kenotic, cruciform love of God, not only within itself, but also in the world, as a foretaste of the final salvation to come.

Summary

Cruciformity, conformity to Christ crucified, is Paul's all-encompassing spirituality, a paradoxical experience of life through death that looks back at the cross and ahead to final salvation. Paul describes this life with God in Christ by the Spirit in three key terms, faith, hope, and love, which together embody the story of Jesus and fulfill the vertical and horizontal requirements of the covenant. To summarize:

- Faith is a total response to the gospel: belief, trust, and sharing in the covenant-fulfilling faithfulness (loyalty) and obedience of Jesus to God the Father, which culminated on the cross.

- Love, as the self-expression of faith, is sharing in the covenant-fulfilling, self-emptying, and self-giving dedication of Jesus to others for their salvation, which culminated on the cross.

- Hope, as the future tense of faith, is the trust-filled conviction that God will soon fulfill all promises and vindicate the faithful; this conviction enables a life of dedication to God (faith) and to others (love) in spite of having to share in the cross of Christ now.

Reflection

1. What does, or what could, "cruciformity" look like in the contemporary context, and how does it, or could it, challenge prevailing understandings of spirituality?

2. Is the Pauline understanding of the cross a "self-as-doormat" interpretation? Can it potentially do harm to minorities or the historically oppressed? How does cruciformity as a *communal* spirituality help us address these issues?

3. What can be done to prevent the common practice of defining faith, hope, and love according to secular visions rather than according to the gospel?

12

"The Glory about to be Revealed"

Return, Resurrection, Renewal

❧ We noted in chapter 5 that "What time is it?" can be a very important spiritual and theological question. As with any story, the story of God and human history raises for us the inevitable question, "How will the story end?" In theological language, reflection on this question is known as the doctrine of "the last things," or *eschatology*. It is obviously very closely related to the spirituality of hope discussed in the previous chapter.

In the truncated, individualistic theology that dominates many forms of Christianity, especially in the West, eschatology means little more than the hope of personal post-mortem survival of the "soul" in a disembodied state in some ethereal paradise called "heaven." In addition, some current versions of the Christian gospel focus on an alleged "rapture"—an unexpected snatching of true Christians from earth that is supposedly taught by Paul.[1] Preoccupation with this invisible coming of Jesus to rescue his own—usually thought to occur before a period of tribulation and then all-out war (Revelation's "Armageddon")—leads many Christians to an escapist mentality and to a dangerous politics that welcomes

---

1. 1 Cor 15:51–58 and especially 1 Thess 4:13–18.

global warming, nuclear proliferation, conflict in the Middle East, and other crises as the fulfillment of biblical prophecy.

Nothing could be further from Paul's rich, thick, hopeful, and cosmic vision of the future than these two misguided scenarios. Paul's vision is a very Jewish one, reworked, of course, in light of Christ. According to Paul, when the new age comes in its fullness, humanity will once again acknowledge God's glory and honor, and God's intention both for humanity, expressed most fully in Christ, and for the entire creation will come to pass. That is what Paul means by "the glory about to be revealed" (Rom 8:18): the coming radiant presence of God in which redeemed humanity and creation as a whole participate forever.[2]

Paul conveys this vision in a variety of ways and images, depending on the context. His expressions of hope draw on a large set of diverse Jewish and Christian traditions, which Paul retrieves and develops primarily to address pastoral needs, like the death of Christians or the denial by some of the resurrection, not to develop rigid chronologies about future realities. Nevertheless, Paul's various versions of his eschatology are all predicated on three major beliefs discussed in chapter 5, namely that:

- in the death, resurrection, and exaltation of Jesus, God has inaugurated the age to come, or new creation, promised by the prophets;

- the inaugurated new age currently overlaps with the present age; and

---

2. See also, similarly, Rev 21:22—22:5.

- in the not-too-distant future, God will act to end the present age and bring the age to come into its glorious fullness.

In this chapter we concentrate on the last of these. Three major sub-themes are woven in and out of the various scenarios in which Paul announces God's future activity: the return of Christ, the resurrection of the body, and the renewal of the creation.

Return: Judgment and Salvation

The New Testament in general, and Paul in particular, affirms what Christians have come to call the "second coming" of Christ. Pauline assemblies prayed *Maranatha*—Aramaic for "our Lord, come!" (1 Cor 16:22). Paul, however, never uses the phrase "second coming"; nor does any other NT writer. Rather, in Paul's letters we find two secular terms that generally refer to the appearance of a royal, imperial, military, or other official figure—*parousia* and *epiphaneia*—and another that refers to a meeting with such a figure—*apantēsis*.[3] So what Paul envisions is something like a "royal appearing" or "official visitation." The Lord who reigns as the true emperor of the world is coming to be greeted by and remain with his people.[4]

Modern Christians who believe in a rapture actually believe in *two* future comings of Christ—the invisible return to rapture the church and the final coming to reign on earth—

---

3. *Parousia*: e.g., 1 Cor 15:23; 1 Thess 2:19; 3:13; 4:15; 5:23; *epiphaneia*: 1 Tim 6:14; 2 Tim 4:1, 8; Tit 2:13; *apantēsis*: 1 Thess 4:17.

4. Paul also makes use of the term *apokalypsis*, or "revelation/revealing" (1 Cor 1:7; 2 Thess 1:7).

although this is never taught in the New Testament and was never heard of in church tradition until very recently.[5] It was created, or at least first widely disseminated, by a nineteenth-century British preacher named J. N. Darby, founder of the Plymouth Brethren and father of the modern rapture-centered belief system.

One popular prooftext for the rapture, 1 Thess 4:13–18, uses two of the terms noted above—*parousia* (appearance) and *apantēsis* (meeting)—along with several traditional apocalyptic images, such as a heavenly trumpet, to portray Jesus' coming. The picture of Jesus coming from heaven and believers meeting him in the clouds reflects the experience of an emperor coming from Rome to a city (the *parousia*) and being greeted outside the city by a delegation from that city (the *apantēsis*). The narrative logic of the image suggests that the emperor and the delegation do not remain in the clouds (outside the city) or return to heaven (Rome) but come to earth—though Paul is not explicit about this. Whatever the specifics of the image may be, the text gives no hint of this appearance being anything other than the final event—the return of Christ and the resurrection of the dead. And Paul never says here, or anywhere else, that the Lord returns to take his people "up to heaven."

The return of Jesus, then, involves the resurrection of the dead, as we will see in more detail below, and thus salvation in

5. The two returns are often thought to be enumerated in Titus 2:13: "while we wait for the blessed hope and the [subsequent] manifestation of the glory [sometimes translated "glorious appearing"] of our great God and Savior, Jesus Christ." But it is more natural (and more consistent with the rest of the New Testament) to see this text as a reference to one final coming.

the form of "the redemption of our bodies" (Rom 8:23)—at least for believers. But the coming of Jesus is also his advent as judge, and his appearance signals not only God's final salvation but also the arrival of the wrath of God (Rom 5:9–10; 1 Thess 1:10; cf. Rom 2:1–16). This combination of judgment and salvation at the *parousia* derives from the prophetic notion of the "day of the Lord," a term that Paul retains (1 Cor 5:5; 1 Thess 5:2; 2 Thess 2:2) but understands as the day of the Lord Jesus/Christ (1 Cor 1:8; 2 Cor 1:14; Phil 1:10; 2:16) and sometimes simply calls "the day" (Rom 13:12; 1 Cor 3:13). It is the "day of redemption" (Eph 4:30) but also the day of wrath/judgment (Rom 2:5, 16).

Judgment and divine wrath are not popular ideas in most modern or postmodern circles. But the image of Jesus as judge is clearly there in Paul, as is the notion of God's wrath (e.g., Rom 2:5–8; 5:9; 12:19; 1 Thess 1:10). The claim that we will all "appear before the judgment seat of God" or Christ (Rom 14:10; 2 Cor 5:10) borrows the image of the public place (*bēma*) where officials evaluated cases and made judgments. Christ's judgment is the judgment of God.

At its core, Paul's teaching on judgment and wrath bear witness to his conviction that God is one who takes evil seriously. Having dealt with evil and sin in the cross and resurrection, God offers new life to all who participate in that cross and resurrection. Those who do not, however, remain in their covenantally dysfunctional state (more graphically, various letters say they are "dead"), alienated from God and from others. Apparently God does not override their desire to remain in that state.

The judgment, Paul believes as a good Jew, will be according to people's deeds (Rom 2:6). Since this seems to contradict the notion of salvation by grace, we must hear Paul carefully, for it does not mean in any sense that salvation is earned. Rather, God's grace operates as a transforming power:

- Life and glory are given to all those who do the good according to their knowledge of it from Jewish law or from conscience (Rom 2:6–16).

- Since, however, people consistently fail to do the good or honor God, being covenantally dysfunctional, God graciously provides a way through Jesus and by the Spirit for people to be reconciled and to fulfill the just requirement of the Law—the essential vertical and horizontal demands of the covenant (Rom 8:3–4 and all of Rom 8:1–17). Grace, as we have seen, is not merely about forgiveness but about transformation—"becoming the righteousness of God" in Christ (2 Cor 5:21).

- God's grace means that those who are in Christ and thus restored to right relationship with God will be spared the coming wrath and will enjoy eternal life (Rom 5:1–11).

- Those who are not in Christ will "perish" (e.g., 1 Cor 1:18, 2:6)—a vague but obviously not positive term.

- All those who are in Christ, and especially those who minister in his name, will be judged and rewarded (in some unspecified sense) according to the character of their activity (1 Cor 3:11–15, 4:1–6; 2 Cor 5:10). The day of Christ is the day of accountability.

The day of Christ is also a day of acclamation; it is the time when "at the name of Jesus every knee should bend, in heaven and on earth and under the earth, and every tongue should confess that Jesus Christ is Lord, to the glory of God the Father" (Phil 2:10–11). Following this universal acknowledgment of Christ as Lord and the end of all his enemies, including Death itself, "the Son himself will also be subjected to the one who put all things in subjection under him, so that God may be all in all" (1 Cor 15:28).[6]

What does all of this mean for those who have not heard or responded to the gospel? As noted above, Paul's references to those who are perishing and to God's judgment do not suggest that he is a universalist—someone who believes all will be saved. Salvation is for all who call upon Jesus as Lord. Salvation is theoretically possible for those who follow their conscience and thereby do good (Romans 2), but no one does good (Romans 3). The waters here are admittedly a bit murky. Paul does, however, have a clear word about the fate of "all Israel": "all Israel will be saved" (Rom 11:26) because "the gifts and the calling of God are irrevocable" (Rom 11:29). Yet even this clear word has engendered considerable debate: Who is all Israel? How will all Israel be saved? When will it occur? These are hotly debated questions. In my judgment, however, the argument of Romans 9–11 as a whole, where Paul discusses this at length, suggests that all Jews will be saved by virtue of God's promise and their acknowledgment of Jesus as Messiah and Lord at his *parousia*, thus finally accepting him as the fulfillment of that divine promise.

6. Paul does not fully articulate the eschatological scenario in one place, so this paragraph must remain a tentative proposal.

Paul thought that the coming of Jesus was imminent (e.g., Rom 13:11–12; 1 Cor 7:29; Phil 4:5), but he did not sit around predicting dates, and he believed it would catch the world, under the illusion of Roman peace and security, by surprise, "like a thief in the night" (1 Thess 5:1–3). Believers, he said, should not be so surprised but should be ready: prepared not by speculating about how and when the *parousia* will occur, but by living lives of faith, hope, and love within their *ekklēsia* and their larger world (1 Thess 5:4–28) and by relativizing all priorities in light of the reality of the present and coming new age (1 Cor 7:25–35). This is the process of becoming whole and holy—and it is the work of God (Phil 1:6, 9–11; 2:12–13; 1 Thess 5:23–28).

Resurrection: Eternal Embodied Life

Most Christians believe that the gift of salvation involves eternal life, and Paul agrees: "For the wages of sin is death, but the free gift of God is eternal life in Christ Jesus our Lord" (Rom 6:23). What does Paul have in mind?

First of all, Paul believes that the death of believers is not the end of their existence but a transformation that has significant continuity with their current reality. Whether alive here or on the other side of death, believers' true purpose is to "live with" Christ (1 Thess 5:10), to please their Lord (2 Cor 5:6–9). But Paul can also view dying as a change from being "in the flesh" or "in the body" to being with Christ, which is a great gain (Phil 1:21–24; cf. 2 Cor 4:14; 5:6–8). To die is to be with Christ in a new and different way, the details of which Paul—unlike many of his later interpreters—refuses to offer.

Second, Paul, like many ancients, compares death to falling asleep; 1 Cor 15:51 and 1 Thess 4:13–15 and 5:10 use this image, though unfortunately many translations render the Greek verb "[fall] sleep" as "die." Paul believes this state of "sleep" is temporary.

Third, Paul clearly holds that all believers will be transformed from an existence characterized by mortality to one marked by immortality. This transformation takes place at the *parousia*; those who are living, or "awake," experience the transformation without dying, while those already dead, or "sleeping," are raised and transformed. Both groups have the same fate:

> [51]Listen, I will tell you a mystery! We will not all die [fall asleep], but we will all be changed, [52]in a moment, in the twinkling of an eye, at the last trumpet. For the trumpet will sound, and the dead will be raised imperishable, and we [the living] will be changed. (1 Cor 15:51–52; cf. 1 Thess 4:13–18).

Fourth, this transformation is also characterized by continuity and discontinuity. In 1 Cor 15:35–50, Paul draws on the existence of different kinds of bodies—earthly and heavenly, for example—and on the analogy of seed being sown in the ground before producing grain, to describe the process of death and resurrection. About the human body ("it," referring to the dead person as an embodied self), Paul says that

> it is sown in dishonor, it is raised in glory. It is sown in weakness, it is raised in power. It is sown a physical body, it is raised a spiritual body. (1 Cor 15:43–44a)

The "it" means continuity of the embodied self, while the notion of different kinds of bodies means discontinuity and transformation. This analogy reinforces what we saw in chapter 8: that when Paul speaks about resurrection, whether Christ's or ours, he is speaking of something that can only be called a resurrection of the body. "He [Christ] will transform the body of our humiliation that it may be conformed to the body of his glory, by the power that also enables him to make all things subject to himself" (Phil 3:21).

It needs to be emphasized again that this is not the same as the resuscitation of a corpse for Christ or for us, since Paul makes it clear that resurrection involves the transformation of the body from its current, perishable character into something different and imperishable. Nevertheless, it is still a *bodily* resurrection, for in line with much Jewish thinking, Paul knew that human beings are a unified whole, a body-soul-sprit, and not merely a soul imprisoned in a physical body longing for release.[7] Much popular Christian spirituality similarly thinks of eternal life as the immortality of the soul apart from the body—a disembodied existence of the "true self." This is very Platonic, but not very Jewish, especially for a Pharisee—and not very Christian, either.[8] Rather, says Paul, the whole self—the embodied self—is transformed. It takes on the quality of what N. T. Wright calls "transphysicality"—referring not to physicality *transcended*, but to physicality *transformed*.[9] The

7. This view was common in Greek thought. The philosopher Plato and his followers believed, for instance, that the body was like a tomb for the soul.

8. For Jewish belief in bodily resurrection, see Levenson, *Resurrection and the Restoration of Israel*.

9. Wright, *Resurrection*, 476–79.

Christian hope is for the redemption of that which has been created—including human bodies.[10]

Although we cannot imagine precisely what this experience will be like, we lose much more than we gain if we deny its bodily character and resort to a lightly Christianized Platonism. Eternal life is about the relationship of embodied selves in unending relationship with God and—one can reasonably argue from Paul's theology—with one another and the rest of creation.

Renewal: The Creation Restored

It is the rest of creation that is our final topic to consider in Paul's eschatology. There are some forms of Christianity, such as those associated with the *Left Behind* series, that see the world as a doomed place, intended for divine destruction. This belief is often a corollary of belief in an escapist, pre-Armageddon rapture and the privatistic immortality of the soul, the very things Paul rejects. Brian McLaren describes it as follows:

> [I]n some versions of the conventional view, the worse the world gets, the better we should feel since salvation—meaning post-mortem salvation after the world is destroyed—is approaching. In too many cases, the conventional view can lead people to

10. Paul makes similar points when he contrasts our "earthly tent" (body) with the "heavenly tent" with which we long to be clothed; the death of believers does not result in being "unclothed" but "further clothed," "so that what is mortal may be swallowed up by life" (2 Cor 5:1–5). Thus the nearby phrase "be away from the body and at home with the Lord" (2 Cor 5:8) should not be read, in context, as expecting a body-less existence.

> celebrate humanity's "progress" in self-destruction
> rather than seeking to turn it around. To put it
> bluntly, in terms of humanity and this earth, the
> conventional view too easily creates—unintention-
> ally, of course—a kind of religious death wish.[11]

Paul, on the other hand, preaches a message of hope that
God the creator is also God the redeemer. While it is true that
"the present *form* of this world [age] is passing away" (1 Cor
7:31; italics added), the One who made the cosmos, including our bodies, will bring the entire creation to its intended
goal—liberation from suffering and death, and participation
in the life and glory of God. Hope for the redemption of the
body is therefore integrally connected in Paul's mind with
hope for the salvation of the entire cosmos, as we saw in the
discussion of Romans 8 in the last chapter (Rom 8:18–25; cf.
Col 1:15–20; Eph 1:8b–10).

Because hope for glory is focused on the unseen, while
what is seen and experienced now is suffering, hope requires
patience (Rom 8:25). Patience recognizes the great difference
between the "slight momentary affliction" and the "eternal
weight of glory beyond all measure" (2 Cor 4:17; cf. Rom
8:18). When the Day comes, not only will suffering cease,
but the ultimate form of suffering, and humanity's worst enemy—Death—will be finally defeated (1 Cor 15:26, 54–57).
The victory of the cross and resurrection will be complete, and
the triumvirate of Sin, the Law (co-opted by Sin), and Death
will be no more (1 Cor 15:54–57).

The patience Paul enjoins, however, is not the passive
patience of the apathetic but the certain confidence of the

11. McLaren, *Everything Must Change*, 82.

committed. It is hope that leads to love, to action, even as faith leads to love. As Paul says to the Corinthians at the very end of 1 Corinthians 15, the conviction that God will be ultimately victorious over suffering, sin, and death leads us to do something here and now: "Therefore, my beloved, be steadfast, immovable, always excelling in the work of the Lord, because you know that in the Lord your labor is not in vain" (1 Cor 15:58).

This is how the age-to-come reaches back into this age: when God's people do God's work in God's way during the overlap of the ages. That is, when they allow the Spirit of the Lord to form them into cross-shaped people who know the resurrection power of God and put it to work in a suffering world that is still waiting in hope for the redemption of our bodies and the liberation of the cosmos. What that looks like specifically must be determined from time to time and place to place. But it is the fruit of hope in the renewal of the cosmos promised by the prophets, fulfilled in Christ, and preached by Paul.

Summary

Gross misunderstanding and misdirected zeal characterize much popular, and even some more sophisticated, theological reflection on the things to come—eschatology. Rightly understood, Paul serves as a corrective. His eschatology focuses on three main dimensions: the return of Christ for salvation and judgment, but without a preliminary rapture; the resurrection of the dead and the transformation of all believers into the presence of Christ for eternal life with God, rather than the body-less immortality of the soul; and the renewal, rather than the destruction, of the cosmos. This is the culmination of Paul's gospel, and of the story of God and human history.

Reflection

1. How do "gross misunderstanding and misdirected zeal" about eschatology negatively affect the practice of Christian faith and the image of Christian faith in the eyes of others?

2. How does the theme of this chapter (eschatology) relate to the theme of the previous chapter (hope)?

3. What contemporary personal, social, and global ethical responsibilities emerge from Paul's eschatological vision and his spirituality of living in hope between Christ's first and second comings?

13

Why Paul? (Reprise)

✣ We began this book by posing the question, "Why Paul?" The basic answer to that question was, "Because Paul speaks *for* God and *to* us"—a bold answer indeed, for all sorts of reasons. A dozen chapters later, we are in a better position to synthesize briefly what Paul said and thus what he might actually be saying to us who read his letters as Scripture nearly 2,000 years later. A good place to start this synthesis is with a review of "Paul in One Sentence," found in chapter 1. Rather than repeat that sentence here, we will try to elaborate on some aspects of it and of the book as a whole.

Before looking specifically at the content of Paul's message for us, however, we can say this about him: Paul calls the church in every age to hear, understand, and perform his gospel—which is really the gospel of God—with courage and imagination appropriate to the specific cultural context in which the church finds itself. The challenge of reading Paul as Scripture, therefore, is that it requires us to read our own context(s) with care and insight, while at the same time allowing Paul's letters to read, question, and challenge us even as we read those letters. This is a strenuous spiritual and theological exercise that requires the guidance of the Spirit.

Having made these general observations about the significance of Paul, we may now consider four dimensions of his gospel that should continue to form us into the community of God's new creation in Christ.

The Character of God

The gospel Paul preaches is first of all about God: God's grace, God's initiative, God's story, God's dream, God's very identity. The God of Paul's gospel is a God of faithfulness and grace, a God who can only be described accurately as "three-in-one," known as Father, Son, and Spirit. The most unexpected aspect of Paul's God-centered good news is that the cross of Christ is revelatory of God; it is, indeed, the definitive theophany. Henceforth, our notions of God's identity and God's attributes, such as divine power and divine love, must be understood in light of the revelatory, redemptive, and reconciling death of Christ on the cross. The God of Paul's gospel is self-giving and self-emptying (kenotic), the one who loves even enemies. This gospel means the end of any form of religion or spirituality that practices power as anything other than self-giving service, and any form of religion or spirituality that defends violence in the name of the biblical God.

God's apocalyptic intervention in Christ is meant to rescue our covenantally dysfunctional human family from its folly of disobedience to God and disregard for neighbor. This kind of rescue operation can only occur by means of God's grace and power because we humans are so blind to our own condition that we think our misguided, self-righteous zeal and our perverted practices of self-satisfaction, contempt, exclusion, and even violence are the will of God. To hear and obey Paul's gospel is to participate in the life of the gracious, faithful, self-giving God by entering into Christ and his body (the church) through the power of the Spirit who gives new life. That is indeed good news.

The Theopolitical Character of the Gospel and the Church

The fundamental confession required by Paul's good news, or gospel, is the acclamation "Jesus is Lord." To make this confession is to make a public, political statement: a pledge of ultimate allegiance that will not allow any individual, people, nation-state, or "-ism" to usurp the role of Jesus as God's appointed Lord and the one to whom we render loyal obedience. The temptations to betray this pledge of allegiance to Jesus are legion. Following Jesus via Paul's gospel means "living with a profound hermeneutic of suspicion toward the 'powers' (Col 1:16; 2:15) that surround us."[1]

Although allegiance to Jesus the Lord is a matter of personal commitment enabled by the Spirit, in chapter 4 we stressed that Paul's gospel "was not a private message of personal salvation, though it included the salvation of individuals." Why? Because it "was a *political* announcement, or better a *theopolitical* announcement (politics involving God), that challenged—and challenges—the very core of how people relate to one another in the real world."[2] In the same chapter, we explained that the use of the word "theopolitical" to describe the gospel means that it is "a narrative about God that creates a public life together, a corporate narrative, that is an alternative to the status quo in the Roman Empire,

1. Page 164.
2. Page 41.

the American empire, or any other body politic."[3] The master story of Christ crucified, raised, and exalted calls into question all other master stories by which people live. In a very real sense, then, to be in Christ is to participate in a subversive community—a *benevolently* subversive community sponsored by a benevolent, saving, redeeming, and restoring God.

In other words, the gospel Paul preaches and the communities his gospel forms by the power of the Spirit are not characterized by a narcissistic obsession with personal salvation as an end in itself, but with a passion for being the obedient people of God in the world, the visible sign that the new age has dawned in the coming of God in Christ. This gospel exposes the "truncated, individualistic theology that dominates many forms of Christianity."[4] It also, quite obviously, makes a huge, transformative impact on all commitments, values, and lifestyles.

Some Marks of the Church

In chapter 3, we noted that Paul was on a mission from God "to spread a powerful word of good news . . . that would establish an international network of transformed, peaceable, multicultural communities worshipping and obeying the one true God by conformity to his Son in the power of the Spirit."[5] This means that the gospel Paul proclaims results in communities with certain essential, evangelical ("gospel") marks; among them are holiness, peaceableness, inclusion, cruciformity, and justice:

3. Page 45.
4. Page 167.
5. Page 22.

- "Holiness" means that the church is called to be a transformed and countercultural community that resists, by walking in the Spirit, the practices of empire and of human, sin-filled normalcy, providing an alternative to the status quo and its distorted values.

- "Peaceableness" means that the church is called to be a community that forsakes violence of all kinds and practices reconciliation within itself and within the wider world. It is rooted in the gospel's central claim, that God in Christ treats enemies with grace, absorbing rather than inflicting violence.

- "Inclusion" means that the church is called to be a multicultural community that expects holiness from all but refuses to define holiness in terms of ethnicity, race, class, or gender.

- "Cruciformity" means that the church is called to a life of Spirit-empowered conformity to Christ crucified as the demonstration of the character and resurrection power of God.

- "Justice" means that the church is called to participate with God in the cruciform, restorative justice (or "righteousness") of God promised by the prophets, brought to fulfillment in Christ, and integral to the experience of justification.

We may summarize these marks of the church in the phrase "bifocal existence in Christ." That is, the church lives in the overlap of the ages with its spiritual eyes constantly focused on both the past event of Christ's death, resurrection, and exaltation and the future event of Christ's *parousia* and

God's redemption of creation. Our life together in and for the world is determined by these two great divine interventions in human history, as we live in the overlap between this age and the age-to-come—which is also where Paul and his congregations lived.

The church, then, is "the countercultural, multicultural community of those justified by God through Christ's cross and living in Christ by the indwelling power of the Spirit."[6] It is a Christophany in and for the world—a living exegesis of the gospel—in fact, of Christ himself!—made possible by walking in the indwelling Spirit, by being in a relationship of reciprocal residence with the crucified and resurrected Jesus.

The Inseparability of Faith, Hope, and Love

The church expresses its character as God's gospel-centered, new covenant people by living in faith, hope, and love. Faith is participation in the cross of Christ that results in trust and loyalty toward God. Just as it was for Christ, love is the self-expression of faith that rejects self-centeredness and acts for the good of the other. And hope is the future tense of faith that grounds our present action in the promise of the coming resurrection of the body and restoration of the entire creation.

Over the centuries, Paul has been called upon to defend both justification by faith alone, often understood very narrowly, and justification that includes deeds. Without in any sense minimizing the role of grace or the need for the Spirit, we have found that one of Paul's great contributions to Christian spirituality, theology, and ethics is his insistence

6. Page 132.

on the inseparability of faith and "works," or faith and love. Paul knows no cheap grace or cheap justification because his experience and understanding of justification are grounded in the cross, understood as Christ's quintessential act of simultaneous faithfulness to God and love for us.

For Paul and for us, there is no faith without love, without action, without compassion and justice. Although James may not have been sure about it (see James 2), Paul and he were quite in agreement on that matter. (Perhaps James, like many others subsequently, had received an incomplete interpretation of Paul.) For us who read Paul as Scripture, "Christian ethics is the resurrection power of the justifying, cruciform, three-in-one God expressing itself as the sign of the cross in daily life."[7]

This kind of loving action, generated by faith, depends ultimately on hope, the conviction that God intends to finish the work of creation known in the stories of Israel and of re-creation revealed in the story of Christ. There is no room for apathy or inaction in the church formed by Paul's gospel—only for the "work of the Lord," knowing that it is "not in vain" (1 Cor 15:58). Such hope is absolutely necessary for the faithful church, for as Paul knew very well, those who are faithful *to* the gospel will likely suffer *for* the gospel. The church or the individual Christian unwilling to accept this reality probably ought not to read the letters of Paul as Scripture.

Conclusion

It would be inappropriate to end a discussion of Paul with a word about suffering that did not put that word in the context

7. Page 130.

of present joy and future glory. Yes, Paul was someone caught up in a mission. Yes, Paul's life-story had a cruciform shape. And yes, Paul regularly suffered for participating in God's mission and Christ's cross. But in spite of this all-consuming passion and its consequences—or perhaps because of it—Paul was someone whose participation in God's new creation was an experience of joy now (Gal 5:22; Philippians), and he was someone whose anticipation of future indescribable joy and glory kept him going (Rom 5:2; 1 Cor 2:9). The pilgrim church on earth that is shaped by his gospel will share that joy and hope, even as we discern how we can participate more fully and faithfully in the same divine mission with Paul-like zeal, courage, and imagination.

Reflection

1. Return to the text of "Paul in One Sentence" in chapter 1. Which aspects of that summary of Paul's message do you now understand more clearly and appreciate more fully? Which aspects do you find particularly germane to the personal, social, spiritual, ecclesial, and political contexts in which you find yourself?

2. Can you interpret the call of Paul to the church described in this chapter in more specific terms for the context(s) in which you and your community are situated? What other elements of Paul's gospel not addressed in this chapter speak to your situation?

Works Cited

Badiou, Alain. *Saint Paul: The Foundation of Universalism*. Translated by Ray Brassier. Cultural Memory in the Present. Stanford: Stanford University Press, 2003.

Barth, Karl. *Church Dogmatics* IV/1: *The Doctrine of Reconciliation*, Part One. Translated by G. W. Bromiley. Edinburgh: T. & T. Clark, 1956.

Bauckham, Richard. *God Crucified: Monotheism and Christology in the New Testament*. Grand Rapids: Eerdmans, 1999.

Bird, Michael F. *The Saving Righteousness of God: Studies in Paul, Justification, and the New Perspective*. Paternoster Biblical Monographs. Carlisle, UK: Paternoster, 2007.

Bonhoeffer, Dietrich. *The Cost of Discipleship*. Rev. ed. Translated by R. H. Fuller. New York: MacMillan, 1959.

Brower, Kent, and Andy Johnson, editors. *Holiness and Ecclesiology in the New Testament*. Grand Rapids: Eerdmans, 2007.

Capes, David B. *Old Testament Yahweh Texts in Paul's Christology*. Wissenschaftliche Untersuchungen zum Neuen Testament 2.47. Tübingen: Mohr, 1992.

Crossan, John Dominic, and Jonathan L. Reed. *In Search of Paul: How Jesus's Apostle Opposed Rome's Empire with God's Kingdom*. San Francisco: HarperSanFrancisco, 2004.

Dawkins, Richard. *The God Delusion*. Boston: Houghton Mifflin, 2006.

Dunn, James D. G. *The New Perspective on Paul*. Rev. ed. Grand Rapids: Eerdmans, 2007.

———. *The Theology of Paul the Apostle*. Grand Rapids: Eerdmans, 1998.

———, editor. *The Cambridge Companion to St Paul*. Cambridge Companions to Religion. Cambridge: Cambridge University Press, 2003.

Elliott, Neil. *Liberating Paul: The Justice of God and the Politics of the Apostle*. 1994. Reprinted, Minneapolis: Fortress, 2005.

Fee, Gordon D. *Empowering Presence: The Holy Spirit in the Letters of Paul*. Peabody, MA: Hendrickson, 1994.

———. *Pauline Christology: An Exegetical-Theological Study.* Peabody, MA: Hendrickson, 2007.

Fitzmyer, Joseph A. *Paul and his Theology: A Brief Sketch.* 2nd ed. Englewood Cliffs, NJ: Prentice Hall, 1989.

Gorman, Michael J. *Apostle of the Crucified Lord: A Theological Introduction to Paul and His Letters.* Grand Rapids: Eerdmans, 2001.

———. *Cruciformity: Paul's Narrative Spirituality of the Cross.* Grand Rapids: Eerdmans, 2001.

———. *Inhabiting the Cruciform God: Kenosis, Justification, and Theosis in Paul's Narrative Soteriology.* Grand Rapids: Eerdmans, 2009.

Green, Joel B. *Seized by Truth: Reading The Bible as Scripture.* Nashville: Abingdon, 2007.

Harnack, Adolf. *History of Dogma.* 7 vols. Translated by Neil Buchanan. 1885. Reprinted, Eugene, OR: Wipf & Stock, 2000.

Harris, Sam. *The End of Faith: Religion, Terror, and the Future of Reason.* New York: Norton, 2004.

———. *Letter to a Christian Nation.* New York: Knopf, 2006.

Harrisville, Roy A. *Fracture: The Cross as Irreconcilable in the Language and Thought of the Biblical Writers.* Grand Rapids: Eerdmans, 2006.

Hays, Richard B. *Echoes of Scripture in the Letters of Paul.* New Haven: Yale University Press, 1989.

———. *The Moral Vision of the New Testament: A Contemporary Introduction to New Testament Ethics.* San Francisco: HarperSanFrancisco, 1996.

Horsley, Richard A., editor. *Paul and Empire: Religion and Power in Roman Imperial Society.* Harrisburg, PA: Trinity Press International, 1997.

Horsley, Richard A., and Neil Asher Silberman. *The Message and the Kingdom: How Jesus and Paul Ignited a Revolution and Transformed the Ancient World.* Minneapolis: Fortress, 2002.

Hurtado, Larry W. *Lord Jesus Christ: Devotion to Jesus in Earliest Christianity.* Grand Rapids: Eerdmans, 2003.

Jervis, L. Ann. *At the Heart of the Gospel: Suffering in the Earliest Christian Message.* Grand Rapids: Eerdmans, 2007.

Levenson, Jon D. *Resurrection and the Restoration of Israel: The Ultimate Victory of the God of Life.* New Haven: Yale University Press, 2006.

Malina, Bruce J., and John J. Pilch. *Social-Science Commentary on the Letters of Paul.* Minneapolis: Fortress, 2006.

McLaren, Brian D. *Everything Must Change: Jesus, Global Crises, and a Revolution of Hope.* Nashville: Nelson, 2007.

Meeks, Wayne A. *The First Urban Christians: The Social World of the Apostle Paul.* New Haven: Yale University Press, 1983.

Sanders, E. P. *Paul and Palestinian Judaism.* Philadelphia: Fortress, 1977.

Segal, Alan. *Paul the Convert: The Apostolate and Apostasy of Saul the Pharisee*. New Haven: Yale University Press, 1990.

Stendahl, Krister. *Paul Among Jews and Gentiles*. Philadelphia: Fortress, 1976.

Swartley, Willard M. *Covenant of Peace: The Missing Peace in New Testament Theology and Ethics*. Grand Rapids: Eerdmans, 2006.

Volf, Miroslav. *Exclusion and Embrace: A Theological Exploration of Identity, Otherness, and Reconciliation*. Nashville: Abingdon, 1996.

Westerholm, Stephen. *Perspectives Old and New on Paul: The "Lutheran" Paul and His Critics*. Grand Rapids: Eerdmans, 2003.

Wright, N. T. *The Climax of the Covenant: Christ and the Law in Pauline Theology*. Edinburgh: T. & T. Clark, 1991; Minneapolis: Fortress, 1993.

———. *Paul: In Fresh Perspective*. Minneapolis: Fortress, 2006.

———. "Paul's Gospel and Caesar's Empire." http://www.ctinquiry.org/publications/wright.htm.

———. *The Resurrection of the Son of God*. Christian Origins and the Question of God 3. Minneapolis: Fortress, 2003.

———. *What Saint Paul Really Said: Was Paul of Tarsus the Real Founder of Christianity?* Grand Rapids: Eerdmans, 1997.

Further Reading

Bassler, Jouette M. *Navigating Paul: An Introduction to Key Theological Concepts*. Louisville: Westminster John Knox, 2007.

Becker, Jürgen. *Paul: Apostle to the Gentiles*. Translated by O. C. Dean Jr. Louisville: Westminster John Knox, 1993.

Beker, J. Christiaan. *Paul the Apostle: The Triumph of God in Life and Thought*. Philadelphia: Fortress, 1980.

———. *The Triumph of God: The Essence of Paul's Thought*. Minneapolis: Fortress, 1990.

Capes, David B., Rodney Reeves, and E. Randolph Richards. *Rediscovering Paul: An Introduction to His World, Letters and Theology*. Downers Grove, IL: InterVarsity, 2007.

Cousar, Charles B. *The Letters of Paul*. Interpreting Biblical Texts. Nashville: Abingdon, 1996.

———. *A Theology of the Cross: The Death of Jesus in the Pauline Letters*. Overtures to Biblical Theology. Minneapolis: Fortress, 1990.

Hawthorne, Gerald F., Ralph P. Martin, and Daniel G. Reid, editors. *Dictionary of Paul and His Letters*. Downers Grove, IL: InterVarsity, 1993.

Horrell, David G. *An Introduction to the Study of Paul*. 2nd ed. New York: T. & T. Clark, 2006.

Murphy-O'Connor, Jerome. *Paul: A Critical Life*. Oxford: Oxford University Press, 1996.

Schnelle, Udo. *Apostle Paul: His Life and Thought*. Translated by M. Eugene Boring. Grand Rapids: Baker, 2005.

Witherington, Ben, III. *The Paul Quest: The Renewed Search for the Jew of Tarsus*. Downers Grove, IL: InterVarsity, 1998.

———. *Paul's Narrative Thought World: The Tapestry of Tragedy and Triumph*. Louisville: Westminster John Knox, 1994.

See also http://bpeterson.faculty.ltss.edu/Paul/bibliography.htm for a very complete bibliography.

Scripture Index

This selective index lists only the most significant texts, especially those discussed and/or quoted at some length.